CONTENTS

FIGURES

To my pupils in schools and colleges, 1944-81

FOREWORD

Teaching 5-13 is a series of books intended to foster the professional development of teachers in primary and middle schools. The series is being published at a time when there are growing demands on teachers to demonstrate increasing levels of professional understanding and competence: Although the importance of personal qualities and social skills in successful teaching is acknowledged, the series is based on the premises that the enhancement of teacher competence and judgement in curricular and organisational matters is the major goals of pre-service and in-service teacher education and that this enhancement is furthered, not by the provision of recipes to be applied in any context, but by the application of practical principles for the organisation and management of learning, and for the planning, implementation and evaluation of curricula. The series aims to help teachers and trainee teachers to think out for themselves ways of tackling the problems which confront them in their own particular range of circumstances. It does this by providing two kinds of books: those which focus on a particular area of the primary or middle school curriculum and those which discuss general issues germane to any area of the curriculum.

Joan Blyth's book deals with a neglected area of the curriculum — the place of 'history' and 'geography' in the education of younger primary school children. She challenges two widely held views: the extreme view that such 'disciplines' can have no meaningful place in the curriculum offered 5 to 9-year-olds, and the less extreme view that incidental learning related to Time and Place will suffice. She has produced a detailed handbook drawing on her own thinking, research and practice, and on a very extensive review of recent literature. The book provides guidelines for the selection and sequencing of content, details approaches and resources and valuably links theory with practice ('warts and all'). Consideration of the arguments she presents, and implementation of some of the many suggestions she puts forward, will enable infant and first schools to counter the criticism made by HMI in *Education 5 to 9* that 'too many schools do too little to draw children's attention to the wider circumstances in which they live or to the past'.

THE SERIES EDITOR

ACKNOWLEDGEMENTS

This book started life as an undertaking between three colleagues. Unfortunately the pressures of College of Education life in the early 1980s forced my two colleagues to withdraw. This proved most difficult in the case of Unit II in Chapter 6, which had to be taught in a school and evaluated. Therefore my gratitude to Mrs Pat Raper, late of Cholsey Infants' School, near Wallingford, is considerable. She quickly and willingly contributed the unit on 'Caves' which she had taught successfully to 5 to 7-year-olds. She also read and commented upon other parts of the book.

I would also like to thank the following people for permission to use copyright material: Alistair Ross for permission to use his ideas on text-books; Croom Helm Ltd for permission to use Figure 3.3 from David Boardman, *Graphicacy and Geography Teaching* (1983); Holt and Saunders Ltd for permission to quote from D.P. Ausubel and P.G. Robinson, *School Learning* (1969); HMSO for permission to use Figure 6.8 from J. Charlton (ed.), *The Tower of London: its Buildings and Institutions* (1978); ILEA History and Social Sciences Teachers' Centre for permission to use material on The Peasants' Revolt; Lawrence Road Infants' School and St Margaret's C. of E. Primary School, Liverpool, for support in my teaching in those schools in 1982; Longmans Group Ltd for permission to adapt material from J. Birt, *The Peasants' Revolt* (1974), J. Sayers, *At the Time of Geoffrey Chaucer* (1977) and M. Reeves, *Why History?* (1980); Macmillan Ltd for permission to use material for Figure 3.2 from G.H. Gopsill, *The Teaching of Geography* (1958); Mersey County Council for permission to use the coat of arms of the Sixth Earl of Sefton (Figure 6.3), through the kindness of Mr E.E. Jackson of Croxteth Country Park; Mrs Hilary Cooper, Mr Ken Maggs and the children of Greenvale Primary School, Croydon, for making the relief model and map in Figure 4.3; Oxford University Press for permission to use Figure 3.1 and Figure 3.7 from E. Barker, *The Junior Geography Lesson* (1960); Paul Noble for permission to use parts of *Time Sense: Curriculum Planning in Primary History* (1981); Routledge and Kegan Paul for permission to use part of J. Forster, *Discovery Learning in the Primary School* (1972); The County of Avon for permission to quote from *History and Geography in Primary Schools: a Framework for the Whole School* (1982); The Director of

Education for Chester for permission to use a poem by David Milligan from *Education in Cheshire* (Autumn, 1985); The Geographical Association for permission to reproduce Figures 2.2, 2.5, 3.4 and 3.5 from David Mills (ed.), *Geographical Work in Primary and Middle Schools* (1981) and Figure 3.6 from J.R. Cracknell, *Teaching Geography through Topics in Primary and Middle Schools* (1979); The Schools Council and the late Mrs Eileen Harries of the London Borough of Merton for help from *The New Approach to the Social Studies*.

Joan Blyth
Liverpool

PREFACE

In different parts of the United Kingdom children between the ages of 5 and 9 are offered various types of school organisation. Since the mid-1960s, the traditional infant and junior school, covering the 5 to 7 and 7 to 11 age-ranges, has been replaced in some LEAs by first and middle schools. In addition, the terms 'first' and 'middle' can mean various age-ranges: thus first means 5 to 8, 5 to 9 or 3 to 9, and middle can mean a multitude of variations up to the age of 14. The pressure of education cuts and reduction in school numbers has led to more 'vertical grouping' in the 5 to 9 age-range, but numbers will increase from 1985 onwards owing to the recent growth in the birth rate. In spite of all these changes in organisation, the actual children to be taught remain the same and have well-defined physical, emotional and intellectual characteristics which are different from older pupils. The unity and continuity of this age-range cannot be over-emphasised; nor can the crucial importance of these years in educational development.

For many years educationalists have not paid serious attention to the place of the environment, near and far, and the past, recent and distant, in the curriculum. There has been a necessary emphasis on the basic skills of language and number which must, of course, continue. Yet young children also need an enlarging of their horizons, and the more able of them are reaching out for stimuli from new challenges. We must ensure that these challenges are planned to give continuity over four years and see that they involve a variety of content and appropriate learning experiences. On account of the paucity of practical and readable books on the themes of Place and Time in the early years, I have written this book in the strongly-held belief that these areas should have a firmer place in the curriculum. In the words of D.P. Ausubel and F.G. Robinson (*School Learning*, Holt, Rinehart and Winston, 1969, pp. 206-7):

> In many of the new curricula there is a tendency to introduce topics in a preliminary way at much younger ages than that at which they were formerly introduced, and with the clear understanding that these topics will be returned to at a later stage... The teacher's task is that of translating ideas into language that is compatible with the child's capacities and level of functioning.

I trust that my efforts will fill a need felt by many trainee-teachers and teachers. Although Place and Time are taught incidentally more frequently than is imagined, they should be approached in a more structured and thoughtful way to avoid repetition of content-matter and to ensure some form of development in learning experiences. Place and Time are integrating factors in a curriculum, and their teaching involves frequent use of a wide range of language strategies, as well as number, and the development of many essential practical skills needed by the time a child is 9 years old.

The book is divided into four parts. The first is concerned with how the disciplines of Geography and History are related to young children; it is also concerned with including them in the curriculum for a multi-racial society. This first section also discusses the selection of subject-matter and how this can be sequenced over the four years. The following most detailed part of the book discusses different approaches to Place and Time in the classroom, and the essential resources specific to them, such as time-lines, globes, maps and information books. In the third part of the book I attempt to show how simple forms of assessment may be used to check on progress. Finally, more detailed specific units of work are tried out and evaluated; these form the last, very practical part of the book, linking content, learning experiences, resources and assessment.

Joan Blyth
Liverpool

Part One

PRELIMINARY THINKING

1 BACKGROUND

The Need for Place and Time in the Curriculum

Work done in the last few years has shown that children between the ages of 5 and 9 can understand Place and begin to understand some aspects of Time, and that 'the past' contains many elements which are not entirely dependent upon an understanding of Time.

All children live in a building in a particular village, town or city and go to school at a particular school. They also watch television and many go on holidays, in this country, if not abroad. Therefore their immediate need for an understanding of Place, and the relationship between different places is very important. This need extends to the use of maps and diagrams, plotting routes and measuring distances and speeds of travel. They should attempt to draw sketch-maps of buildings, places and transport facilities such as roads and railways. In order to do these things it is important to develop careful observation on visits and field excursions. In addition the concept of scale is important, as even older juniors can easily become confused by pictures of buildings and towns if there is no comparison of size. Natural curiosity, the need for racial tolerance and the widening of horizons from the purely local environment are satisfied by the study of places near and far. The constant factor of weather and climate in all our lives, and the way this controls what we do is better understood by learning from an early age.

Although these are basic needs for all geographers and are developed in the later junior and secondary years, most children aged 5 to 9 are interested to be initiated into the wonders of the local environment, globes and maps, and to find out how people live in other lands. Those who believe in J.S. Bruner's 'spiral curriculum' will agree that these ideas can, and should, be taught in an appropriate way from the age of 5.

Infants and younger juniors are usually taught to 'tell the time', using large clock-faces with movable hands and utilising their increasing familiarity with number (particularly up to number 12). It is a necessary life-skill to be able to read a clock or watch correctly. The duration of a day can lead to understanding of 'yesterday' and 'tomorrow', a week, a month and so on. But young children need help with this extension of clock-time to real time, from a numerical understanding to a conceptual one. It is here that a teacher of the past is so useful. This extension of

3

time involves the understanding of sequence, that is, the ordering of events, the age of people and objects, language (such as 'old' and 'century'), actual historical dates (and how they differ from telephone numbers), and the whole concept of the past and how different it is from the present. Children between 5 and 9 need to begin to grapple with these larger aspects of time.

In addition it should be borne in mind that 'the past' is not only a time dimension. It is concerned with real people of many different ages and nationalities, and both sexes, living between prehistoric and contemporary man. It is also concerned with events great and small, ranging from a family event such as a birthday party, to the Armada of 1588 or the Second World War. Above all the past is how real people and real events interact. It helps to explain ourselves, our families and our present environment; it answers the perennial question — 'Why are we like we are and in our present situation?' The past is also the source which gives us evidence about our ancestors, and our interpretation of these clues. The fact that these sources are often incomplete is itself a lesson for life to be learnt by children. These parts of the past do not require conceptualisation as in the case of time but instead finding out information, remembering, imagination and discussion for understanding.

If these essentials of place and time in their broadest sense are married to the development of the child between the ages of 5 and 9 they are found to be needed for his or her satisfactory development. During this age-range children are developing very quickly physically, from babies to children. They have abundant energy for field work and are gaining in powers of manipulation and control in handling artefacts and writing about them. Intellectually they require the stimulus of story, the satisfying of curiosity about the world, the wider use of books and pictures and above all talking about their work with teachers and peers. They need the 'decentring'[1] of their minds from themselves to other things, and the experience of working co-operatively in a small group and, if possible, a large one. Emotionally they need to be helped to be unselfish, self-controlled and confident. This book hopes to illustrate how the past in its broadest sense can feed these needs and create a more stable yet sensitive 9-year-old.

The Contribution of Other Studies

Having established the need for Place and Time in the first school, the contribution of research projects and literature may help us to formulate a more positive role for those areas in the curriculum. Neither the Schools Council, nor any other funded organisation thought fit to give money for research into Place and Time in relation to very young children during the expansive years of the 1960s and early 1970s. This is evidence enough for our lack of information, and the need for some work to be done in this area.

I will consider four research projects, some of which are concerned with other areas of the curriculum, but which, nevertheless, have implications for Place and Time. They are *The Nuffield Junior Science Project* (1963-6), *The Schools Council Environmental Studies Project 5-13* (1969-72), *The Schools Council Communication Skills Project 3-11* (1971-6) and *The New Approach to the Social Studies* of the London borough of Merton for the Schools Council (1977-80). In addition there is Dr John West's individually-directed research into History in Dudley schools (1974-80) with children aged 7 to 11.[2] With the exception of Dr West's work the researchers presume that Place and Time are treated 'topically', thus avoiding the planned structure needed to teach even the basic elements of Time. More will be said about the content of this planned structure as it is seen in the second chapter of this part of the book.

Nuffield Junior Science published a pamphlet *Science and History* (Collins 1967) showing how the two disciplines could be linked through 'discovery learning'. Stories of great scientists could be told in story time and topics such as 'Cavemen', 'Voyages of Discovery' and 'Transport' could link the two disciplines in many ways, it suggested. Stories about cavemen lead to discussion on such topics as making fire, using vegetable dyes, tie-dying and the effect of water on dry clay. This type of work is suggested for 7 to 8-year-olds and would demand considerable preparation on the part of the teacher.[3] *Science 5-13*, a much larger undertaking, is also in favour of almost undiluted 'discovery learning' particularly through practical experience leading to questions, discussion and more activities. The Guide to the Project, *With Objectives in Mind* (Macdonald, 1972) shows a photograph of a model of a wattle and daub wall made by juniors with the caption 'Science or history: does it matter?'. Yes, it does matter, for those interested in the teaching of Time are very much concerned with the stage of man's existence when he made these walls and how this stage is related to other stages. Historians go one step further and want to order experiences into a *time* structure. This project, very enthusiastically received in primary schools, has published units of work on *Time, Early Experiences, Changes, Ourselves, Holes, Gaps and Cavities* and *Using the Environment*, all of which provide very close links with Time and its broader elements. The chart of objectives given at the back of the guide to the project shows them all to be relevant to a study of Place and Time.

The Schools Council Environmental Studies Project 5-13 was directed by Melville Harris and used Welsh and English schools for its practical purposes. It emphasised Place more than Time, possibly because it was led by a geographer. It may have helped to influence many primary schools to think that all Place and Time could be catered for by the local environment. Yet the project did say that Environmental Studies should not be studied for the whole year by any class since many children already knew their own environment and want to study pastures new and further afield, even as early as 8 to 9. The project emphasised the need for children to understand how to use pictures, diagrams and maps even more than books, and to begin to develop the study skills of collecting, classifying, testing, mapping and interpreting photographs. For example, they should be able to compare two photographs of one area at different stages of time and to list the differences. *Reasons* for these changes are really the work of upper juniors. Comparison was also made by young children going on walks in their own areas and looking at an old parish church and its gravestones, a home for elderly residents, a 1776 public house and derelict factories. Young children were also encouraged to use portable tape-recorders to record the talk of old people, people doing different jobs (milkman, postman etc.) and the sounds of the environment. Although this project was conducted at the height of the post-Plowden 'discovery' period and presumed that all Place and Time were studied in Topics, it warns of the 'serious disadvantages' of the school having no overall policy. This project favours a school policy based on skills. In spite of the popularity of the 'integrated day', especially for the 5 to 9 age-range it stipulates the need to set aside two afternoons a week for six weeks for an Environmental Study to be worthwhile.

Dr Joan Tough, of the University of Leeds, directed a very big Schools Council Project on *Communication Skills 3-11*, at first being concerned with children in nursery schools and then infant schools, with some interest in the whole primary range. This work is helpful to Place and Time because it is concerned with language and all communication skills, although no geographical or historical material is used. The main argument of this project is that young children need to talk to teachers and to each other for them to develop concepts and make progress in learning. Examples are given showing that less able children and those from disadvantaged homes need planned discussion with teachers to make the same progress in learning as more verbally fluent children. In the age-range of 5 to 7 particularly, children find reading and writing difficult and talking is their main means of communication. This project shows in *Listening to Children Talking*[4] that children can use language for 'reporting on present and past experiences, logical reasoning, predicting and anticipating possibilities, projecting into the experience of others and building up an imaginative scene for play through talk'.[5] All these uses for language are fulfilled by talking with children involved in discussion of geographical and historical materials. By the time children are 7 they are able to talk about what they have learnt beyond themselves as well as about themselves and their immediate environment. Joan Tough comments: 'it would seem that history and literature. . . are dependent on ways of thinking that are similar in character to those being developed in imaginative play'.[6] This project shows very usefully how pictures and 'interesting objects' can be used for talking and learning; it can be used to teach about the past and about different places by supplementing historical and geographical pictures and objects for discussion. Although not as directly useful as her first book, *Talking and Learning,*[7] it develops the Project's theme further. It shows how children can use talking to 'recall past experiences' more readily and to enter into 'the feelings of others'.[8] By recalling their own past experiences and entering into the feelings of people around them they are more able to recall experiences of the life of people of the past and to try and enter into their feelings. Recall and 'sympathy' are two important parts of being able to understand and enjoy the past. Thus communication through oral work is a vital factor in learning about Place and Time.

More pertinent to the work of this book is a recent piece of research done in the London Borough of Merton under the leadership of the Humanities Adviser, Eileen Harries. In *The New Approach to the Social Studies*[9] continuity and development in children's learning was studied in first, middle and high schools, drawing extensively on the ideas of the *Schools Council History, Geography and Social Science Project 8-13*[10] which used Merton schools for trials. We should wholeheartedly agree with this viewpoint from Merton: 'It is in the first school that the foundations of all aspects of pupils' learning are laid. They need foundations not only in language and mathematics but also in social studies . . . while all these disciplines have much in common, *each has its own distinctive contribution to make* to children's understanding of social affairs.'[11] My italics emphasise that in this book I am concerned with how children need the specific disciplines of Geography and History at their own level. Thus I entirely endorse the Merton approach suggesting that we need to integrate at times yet maintain separate elements at others. Examples of separate treatment are given for 8-year-olds in 'Pompeii' and 'The Elizabethan Age' in the Merton study. The project emphasises the changes in the teaching and learning of Geography at all levels during the last twenty years. This involves teaching concepts, patterns and the influence of social environmental issues rather than facts about regions and their peoples. It also puts great stress on direct experience for younger children through field work. A course unit of an inter-disciplinary nature on 'The Neighbourhood' is given as a first school example. The Appendix has a helpful scheme on how to develop mapping skills; young children should draw maps of their classrooms, the school and school grounds and finally be able to use a large-scale map of the local area.

Although the Merton project was more concerned with ways of thinking, use of evidence and development of concepts rather than suggestions for schemes of work, it was found in most schools that there was 'a dearth of resources associated with lack of a planned approach'.[12] All first schools in an area are advised to agree upon schemes so that middle schools know what ground has been covered by the age of 9; the same applies to infant and junior schools.

The most specific historical work has been done by Dr John West.[13] Although his large-scale research was done with 7 to 11-year-old children, preliminary work with 6-year-olds was of considerable importance. A variety of historical artefacts (such as prehistoric tools or a Victorian sampler) were handled and discussed with 6-year-olds. The children were asked to identify them, deduce certain assumptions from them and place them in sequence of historical time. It was found that these children had a strong time-sense, strong powers of deduction and precise powers with words to describe the objects. Their knowledge was naturally more limited. Work with 7 and 8-year-olds over the period 1976-80 used History stories, museum objects and narrative pictures with constant reference to time-lines and time-charts. Dr West's aim was to find out how much perception of evidence (How do we know?), authenticity (Is it genuine or true?) and age (including sequence in chronology, difference and change) the children had. One group of 7-year-olds could not only put the prehistoric tools into time-sequence but could name appropriate modern tools for comparison. Powers of observation were very high in the 6 to 8-year-olds who also showed curiosity about the past and had a considerable feel for it. In common with Dr Tough's work on language, increase of understanding came from children talking with teachers and with peers, using phrases such as 'long, long ago' and 'recent' correctly. Duration of time was beyond the understanding of 8-year-olds but Dr West has found a coherent development of historical skills and attitudes during the primary years.

No authoritative book has been published on Place and Time in the first school but valuable articles have appeared in journals during the last decade.[14] The Bibliography at the end of the book refers to the more useful articles. Psychologists and educationalists interested in these early years have contributed useful ideas which can be associated with Place and Time, though little help has yet been given to teachers as to how this should be done. Jean Piaget's stages of intellectual development do not encourage teachers of Place and Time, since the 'pre-operational' and 'concrete operational' stages usually associated with 5 to 9-year-olds do not point to concept formation.[15] Yet much of Piaget's research was in the scientific area and he has had several critics as far as the social subjects are concerned. Teachers trained to rely heavily on Piaget's views can easily dismiss the teaching of Place and Time as impossible. Psychologists working since Piaget's early researches have found that all children do not go through stages of mental development at the same time and that good teaching can in fact hasten them. For example, Peter Bryant found that 4 to 6-year-olds could make inferences from knowledge if they could remember the knowledge[16]; he emphasised that training in memory was needed to overcome this lapse. Margaret Donaldson[17] rejected 'certain features of Jean Piaget's theory of intellectual development' in that children's minds are more like adults' than has been thought and their reasoning depends upon teachers giving them 'real-life' experiences in the very early years, enabling them to 'decentre' and extend their interest from themselves.

A broader band of workers includes educationalists who use the findings of psychologists to help the teaching of individual academic disciplines. Professor J.S. Bruner has had considerable influence on teachers of social subjects as his idea of a 'spiral curriculum' is more optimistic than previous viewpoints. He emphasises the need to teach the 'structure' of a subject rather than a certain piece of knowledge, and believes that all knowledge can be taught at all stages of intellectual development if done from the child's point of view. Thus young children should be taught about the attack of the barbarians on Rome from the story of how the geese saved Rome[18] rather than by a study of Edward Gibbon's *Decline and Fall of the Roman Empire* in several volumes. Children should be encouraged to ask questions and have 'hunches' in their problem-solving, not expecting always to 'reach the right answer'. Under these conditions Place and Time can be taught and over-doses of facts, names and dates avoided. P.J. Rogers has applied Bruner's ideas to History teaching in a number of publications.[19] He does not oppose the teaching of History to 5 to 9-year-olds but warns teachers to limit the coverage of the material they use and to concentrate on concrete objects from which to learn.

Another educationalist/historian, Kieran Egan, thinks that children between the ages of 5 and 9 are going through the 'mythic stage' of their development and that true stories from the past as well as myths are essential to feed their minds. He gives examples of how to construct stories from 'The Story of Civilisation' and 'North American Indians'. He believes that the exclusion of Place and Time from the curriculum in these years can never be rectified.[20]

Many LEAs are trying to help teachers with guidelines for different areas of the curriculum since the publication of the HMI Primary School Report in 1978. The ILEA has been able to publish guidelines in History, Geography and Social Studies. Many teachers all over the country are finding *History in the Primary School* and *The Study of Places in the Primary School* very helpful.[21] In a most succinct summary of 'the concept of time' in the first publication (page 6) we learn that 5 to 7-year-old children should be able to put the events of the past in sequence, that by the age of 8 children see the past as different from the present, but up to 9 they can only understand the recent past (sixty years back, which is up to two generations). During this First School period they should be gradually acquiring historical vocabulary and using words like 'generation', 'decade', 'century' and 'reign'. Understanding duration of time develops in the upper junior years. This pamphlet emphasises the need for a chronological framework through the primary years and the necessity for the use of sequence/ time lines.

The Study of Places in the Primary School is a happy combination of very practical advice, sound scholarship in curriculum development and much experience. It is also a most attractively presented publication and should be the basis of Place and Space work in the First School. The authors have the philosophy of the need for continuity from age 5 to 11 and therefore for planning for teachers. They base their ideas on the work of Professor J.S. Bruner, already mentioned.

Thus they emphasise that most geographical concepts can be taught from an early age and repeated in different ways as age advances. This 'spiral curriculum' is illustrated by a diagram of how 'housing' can be taught to 5-year-olds and 18-year-olds. The most impressive part of the publication is the very clear matrix showing how experience (direct or indirect) and graphicacy (maps and other aspects) can be taught between 5 and 11. Useful lists of books for children and for teachers make the pamphlet an excellent investment for those teaching Geography and Environmental Studies in the primary school.

A less ambitious but very relevant pamphlet has been produced by the County of Avon, *History and Geography in Primary Schools; a Framework for the Whole School.*[22] It is mainly concerned with helping individual schools to construct a syllabus and it emphasises the need to have a school policy on Place and Time known to all staff and to give one staff member responsibility for implementing it. Important working papers, yet to be published, will form the second part of these guidelines: 'Maps and Mapwork in the Primary School', 'The Language of Place and Time' and 'Teaching about other Places and People' are some of the forthcoming titles.

The two government surveys, *Primary Education in England* (1978) and *Education 5 to 9: an Illustrative Survey of 80 First Schools in England* (1982) show us how much Place and Time are the Cinderellas of the curriculum in all but a few schools, and offer suggestions for improvement. The general situation showed lack of planning and superficial standards, able children not being sufficiently extended and work being repeated often at the same level. Maps were used in many schools but not usually as early as 8 years old and globes were almost unknown. In the 1982 Report, Time is known as 'Learning about People' (including 'People in Other Times') and Place as 'Learning about the Physical World' (including maps, globes, models and weather). As in the 1978 report lack of planning is at the heart of the problem, leading to lack of any idea of chronology in Time and spasmodic use of maps and globes in Place. Little work on the past was done at all in the 5 to 8 age-range, not even the use of artefacts or the memories of older people. Good work was done in some 5-to-9 schools on 'weather' and 'the sea-shore'. Both these reports point to the need for consultant specialists in First Schools, since many of the shortcomings can be attributed to lack of knowledge and experience rather than purposeful omissions.

What do we, as teachers, learn from all this theory and writing? We learn that Place and Time are low priorities in schools for children aged

5 to 9, and when work is done on either or both of them it is due to the inspiration of the exceptionally gifted and/or enthusiastic individual teacher, not to any overall policy of a school, LEA or the DES. Secondly, we learn that these outstanding examples could be used as a basis to help others if publicity and communications were improved. Thirdly, we learn that Place and Time should be considered in a wider orientation than the purely local (Environmental Studies) or even national; they must have a 'world' connotation as early as the ages of 5 to 9. Lastly we learn that very young children can understand more difficult work than hitherto expected and reach a good standard in it if the appropriate methods are used by their teachers.

Aims and Objectives in Place and Time

When teaching geographical and historical material to children aged 5 to 9 we are trying to start them off on an understanding of Place and Time to be built upon in their later schooling. This understanding and also knowledge applies equally to the well-known place or locality in which they live and to the wider 'place' of other areas in their own country and some others. In the same way it applies to an understanding of sequence of events, what happened before what, both in their own lives and in the lives of other people living in the past. This should lead by the age of 8 or 9 to some knowledge of historical chronology involving outstanding dates such as 1066 (Norman Conquest), 1588 (the Armada), 1837 (the accession of Queen Victoria) and 1939 (the outbreak of the Second World War).

These are the wider aims of Place and Time and in order to carry them out children should be able to *do* certain things. Both areas of the curriculum demand close observation of surroundings and people and therefore involve going out of school, near and far (Environmental Studies). Both need the ability to read pictures accurately and, if possible, appropriate books, finding information, for example, using the index and contents page of a book. The ability to make a record by drawing a rough diagram, plan or sketch-map, and use a map, is needed by both disciplines, particularly Place (graphicacy). Time is particularly concerned with evidence, especially evidence to be seen and heard (oral evidence of older people). Place and Time have their own language and a beginning should be made to build up vocabulary lists such as 'volcano', 'basin', 'meadow', 'century', 'decade', 'manor' and 'royalty'. Above all during these years teachers should be encouraging delight in talking about Place and Time and listening to others doing the same. This interest cultivated in the earliest years is the greatest boon to children for their later schooling as well as leisure pursuits in later life.

Notes

1. M. Donaldson, *Children's Minds* (Fontana, 1978), pp. 17-31.
2. J. West, 'Children's Awareness of the Past', unpublished PhD thesis, Keele University, 1981.
3. The Teaching Unit II on 'Caves' in Chapter 6 is an example.
4. J. Tough, *Listening to Children Talking* (Ward Lock, 1976).
5. Ibid., p. 78, where these uses of language are presented in note form.
6. Ibid., p. 79.
7. J. Tough. *Talking and Learning* (Ward Lock, 1977).
8. Ibid., p. 22.
9. *The New Approach to the Social Studies* (London Borough of Merton, 1981) from London Borough of Merton, Station House, London Road, Morden.
10. *Place, Time and Society. An Introduction* (Collins/ESL, 1975).
11. *The New Approach to the Social Studies*, p. 9.
12. Ibid., p. 16.
13. J. West. *Awareness of the Past*; 'Young Children's Awareness of the Past' in *Trends in Education*, Spring Issue 1 (1978); 'Primary School Children's Perception of Authenticity and Time in Historical Narrative Pictures', *Teaching History*, no. 29 (February, 1981); 'Testing the Use of Written Records in Primary Schools', *Teaching History* no. 32 (February 1982); J. Lally and J. West. *The Child's Awareness of the Past, Teachers' Guide* (Hereford and Worcester County History Committee, 1981).
14. *Teaching History* from the Historical Association, 59A Kennington Park Road, London SE11; *Teaching Geography* from the Geographical Association, 343 Fulwood Road, Sheffield S10 3BP; *Education 3-13*, Studies in Education Ltd., Nafferton, Driffield, North Humberside YO25 0JL.
15. R.M. Beard, *An Outline of Piaget's Developmental Psychology for Students and Teachers* (RKP, 1969).
16. P.E. Bryant, *Perception and Understanding in Young Children* (Methuen, 1974).
17. M. Donaldson, *Children's Minds* (Fontana, 1978) p. 9.
18. F. Saxey, *Classical Stories* (OUP, 1968).
19. P.J. Rogers. *The New History: theory into practice* (Historical Association, T.H. 44 1979).
20. K. Egan, *Educational Development* (OUP, 1979) pp. 21-5; K. Egan. 'Teaching the varieties of History', *Teaching History*, no. 21 (June 1978).
21. *History in the Primary School* (ILEA Guidelines, 1980); *The Study of Places in the Primary School* (ILEA Guidelines, 1981).
22. *History and Geography in Primary Schools* (Avon LEA, 1982) from Weston Teachers' Centre, Westcliff, Kewstoke Road., Weston-super-Mare BS23 2CR.

2 APPROACHES TO CONTENT: WHAT PLACE AND TIME?

Does Content Matter?

Is there specific knowledge which children aged 5 to 9 need which they will not get in future schooling? Are these years, so vital in a child's development, also fundamental in his understanding of Place and Time? These and many other questions are asked by teachers trying to formulate either an integrated or separate subject scheme for their school, with or without guidelines from an LEA or anywhere else.

Yet both the 1978 HMI Primary Report and the 1982 *Education 5 to 9* Report insist that planning for the whole span of years is sadly lacking and 'a framework is required'. Content *does* matter, if only as a conveninent vehicle for teaching concepts, skills and attitudes. This requires reading and knowledge on the part of the teacher. Content is closely related to methods and resources and only the over-bold teacher will embark on a scheme of work which denies her use of correct methods or for which she cannot provide appropriate activity for her class.

Whether we like it or not the thorny question of content has got to be grasped for continuity to be pursued and to avoid an unhealthy repetition of work done at the same standard over the four years. Organisational problems must be taken into consideration, since many areas have infant and junior schools whereas others have first (5 to 8 or 5 to 9) and middle schools (8 to 12 or 9 to 13). This means that each school must decide on its own scheme in consultation with others in the district. The 5 to 7 age-range, when basic skills are being mastered, may be considered on its own. Place and Time may be taught as separate disciplines or in an integrated framework in the 7 to 9 age-range, dependent upon the needs of the school and the feelings of the staff. It may be better to develop the basic skills of Place and Time in the earlier years and use them for an integrated environmental scheme in the later years. This might seem a sensible idea as integration is more difficult to teach and learn. I shall consider both separate and integrated (or interrelated) schemes in this part of the book.

Both in Place and Time there was little direct assistance or choice of scheme for teachers until about 1980 (when it was demanded by the 1978 HMI Report). Therefore the non-specialist teacher had to depend on the four-stage textbook series, which tended to become a scheme sometimes inappropriate to a particular school, because not tailor-made for it. Thus *New Ways in Geography* by J.P. Cole and N.J. Benyon (Blackwell, 1969) and *Looking at History* by R.J. Unstead (A. and C. Black, 1950 and following years) became the staple diet for many junior schools, if any books were used at all. Even then *New Ways in Geography* was written for 9 to 11-year-old pupils.

Certain basic principles should guide both Place and Time studies in the 5 to 9 age-range, whether the scheme is separate subject teaching or interrelated. Figure 2.1 summarises them.

Figure 2.1: Basic Principles for Place and Time

Type of Work	Place	Time
Ever-present stable background of scheme	Plans, maps and globes	Sequence/time-lines; understanding of chronology
Local	Near places to visit	Near places, related to the past, to visit
The World	Distant lands to see, hear talk and read about	Distant places in the past to see, hear, talk and read about

Globes, maps and time-lines should constantly be referred to, and, although appearing to be a method of teaching, they are essentially the controlling factors for all schemes, however selective, and must form an integral part of any 5 to 9 age scheme. If these basic tools of Place and Time are not learnt as soon as possible, however slowly and painfully, the rest of the scheme will become pointless, lacking in unity and deteriorating into 'bits of information' offered to young children at random, when the spirit moves the teacher and the class.

Schemes for Place and Time in the 5 to 7 Age-range

Until quite recently — during the last five years — geographers and historians did not encourage teachers of 5 to 7-year-old children to work out any pattern for their use of Place and Time in the curriculum. This reticence was accepted by infant teachers and trainers of infant teachers as in keeping with their desire to concentrate on number, language, physical education and creative work in these early years. The 1982 HMI Report, *Education 5 to 9*, supports the need for Place and Time to be an integral part of the curriculum. It says 'guidelines . . . are urgently needed . . . especially in geography, history and science'.[1] This Report reflects a growing awareness amongst teachers of young children that the more able children need to be stretched by the 'information' areas of the curriculum and that all children will benefit from appropriate experience of Place and Time. I have recently come across one LEA which prefers First Schools to teach depth topics in History, Geography and Science, and Middle Schools to undertake integrated work. This appears to be working well in this authority.

The Geographical Association puts forward ideas, topics and activities in *Geographical Work in Primary and Middle Schools*.[2] This publication gives a very 'outline' structure for Place as a separate subject and does not detail how much time should be spent on each topic or where it should be taught in the school year. It does emphasise that all four 'key ideas' of physical studies, local environment, distant areas, and other topics should appear in both years, and that the use of maps should start in these years. The activities suggested in outline in this scheme are explained in detail in later chapters of this Geographical Association publication. The scheme is given in Figure 2.2.

In a previous publication I have argued a case for a separate Time scheme in the 5 to 7 age-range.[3] Subsequent reading, thinking and discussion with teachers and my own teaching have to some extent revised this scheme. During the first two terms of the first year when children enter most schools in September, January and in April, no sequential work is possible. Therefore I now recommend for these two terms 'Stories from the Past', though it is possible to group a month's stories round one historical figure (e.g. St Francis of Assisi) or topic. I do not now favour 'Myths and Legends' during these early terms. In their third term of the first year children could gain their first concrete experience of historical evidence by handling and discussing artefacts/old objects brought by the teacher initially and then by themselves. They should go back in time as far as possible and the teacher may have to borrow artefacts from the local museum to see any before about 1900. More continuous work can be undertaken in the second year when the class group is more settled. A ten-week study of family history could start with 'life-lines' of the teacher, or an imaginary person, and the children, followed by family-plans (or family-trees) of the same people. This could develop into the collecting of family photographs and artefacts, culminating in a display. Stories of families

Figure 2.2: A Suggested Structure for Geographic Work for 5-7s

Some Key Ideas	Some Suggested Topics/Themes	Some Activities
Physical studies Weather affects us	Weather studies (stress relationship with children's activities)	Using simple weather instruments Simple recording
Local Environment Plans, shape, texture, movement Growth and change Water and land	Local work on houses, shops, streets; traffic in street, movement of pupils in school, local gardens, parks and open spaces	Observation Measuring, recording collecting, sorting Making models Use map of local area
Distant areas Other places in Britain are different from local environment	Work based on visits	Reading Looking at photographs
Other places in the world are different from the British environment	Homes of children/animals of other lands	Writing Simple plans Making models
Others (examples) Differences between day and night	What animals/plants/people do by day and night	Make graphs/charts Classification
Differences between the seasons	Spring, Summer, Autumn, Winter	Collage and model making Collecting

Key Resources
Globe.
1:2,500, 1:10,000 maps for teacher

Figure 2.2 (Continued)

Summary

By the end of the Infant School the children should have:

1. undertaken some work in the local environment, e.g. local streets, shops, houses, park, water;
2. drawn simple maps of classroom and local area;
3. made simple weather measurements in order to understand that weather changes from day to day;
4. undertaken studies to show that different areas of Britain and the world look and are different from their own home area.

Source: D. Mills (ed.), *Geographical Work in Primary and Middle Schools* (Geographical Association, 1981), p. 13.

in the past[4] and stories from visiting grandparents and old friends should also form part of the work. The second and third terms of the second year might well be spent on appropriate topics of very local history and visits to one or two of these places. This could be treated in a regressive scheme (working backwards in time) from 1983 to 1837, with one patch on earlier times if resources gave information on medieval (up to about 1500) or Tudor history. Stories could be read or told about important personalities of the period studied (e.g. Queen Victoria) and the oral history of an older person could again be used. This should also end with a display of local work and visits. In studying the local area simple map work would have to be undertaken, so integrating Place into the work.

As already mentioned, Avon LEA has published, mainly for its own teachers, a scheme of interrelated work on Place and Time.[5] This scheme does not specify in which part of the 5 to 7 age-range the topics should be studied, but it does give examples of how 'basic graphical and historical skills' may be taught through the selected topics. This loose topic approach in which Place and Time can be treated naturally, and interrelated if appropriate, will appeal to many teachers of younger primary children. The Avon scheme is given in Figure 2.3.

Using the experience of these separate and interrelated schemes for the 5 to 7 age-range I have evolved an integrated scheme of Place and Time which might suit some schools. In this scheme more emphasis is put on Place in the first year although there are the constant factors of stories from the past and artefacts throughout the two years. According to the interests of teachers, more emphasis could be placed on Time in the second year, although the visits and map work in the second and third terms might emphasise Place more for some teachers. In this scheme Place and Time would not necessarily be studied throughout each term. The second year needs more continuity of teaching as it is a scheme showing development, and the second and third terms are closely linked, the second being a preparation for visits in the third. A child working on this scheme would be well prepared for Place/Time work in the junior school. My integrated Place/Time scheme is given in Figure 2.4.

Schemes for Place as a Separate Area of the Curriculum in the 7 to 9 Age-range

In agreement with the HMI 1978 Report, Roger Cracknell believes that even the act of planning a course on Place, whether separate or inter-

Figure 2.3: History/Geography Syllabus: Infants

	Autumn Term	Spring Term	Summer Term	Development of Basic, Graphical and Historical Skills
Lower Infant	Where we live – different types of homes today and yesterday Our school Streets: names, size, the Fosseway	Shops, churches and other places of interest Where people work, past and present	Animals of the desert and the jungle	Language work number work vocabulary extension (a checklist at the end of each term to show words introduced) Concept of space through drawing mental maps; simple diagrams; street models; use of globes/maps when relevant, stickers showing where children have visited, have relations or an area under discussion; empathy
Upper Infant	Our climate and weather		A far-away place e.g., family life in India	Concept of time through time-lines (again use of stickers); family-trees; empathy

Source: from *History and Geography in Primary Schools* (Avon LEA, p. 15)

Figure 2.4: Integrated Place and Time Scheme for 5-7s

	Term 1	Term 2	Term 3	Constant factors
Age 5-6	Animals of desert and jungle	A far-away place, e.g. family-life in India	Our school, street and traffic 'Farm Study' (link with terms 1 and 2) or 'The Seashore' (visits in all cases)	Stories of the past; artefacts as evidence; weather; maps; differences between day and night: the seasons; left-hand/right-hand; points of the compass
Age 6-7	Homes, today and yesterday; family history (artefacts) Stories of families in the past	Local topics shops, parks, stream/river, churches, historic buildings, other places of interest, work places, past and present (visits and simple maps/diagrams)		

disciplinary, leads to more time being spent on Geography in the primary school. He further thinks that poor emphasis on geographical skills has led to inadequate map work, and poor provision of resources has further limited good teaching. He quotes John Dewey to support his viewpoint: 'It is ground for legitimate criticism when the ongoing movement of progressive education fails to recognise that the problem of selection and organisation of subject-matter for study and learning is fundamental.'[6] Thus Dewey emphasised the importance of correct subject matter for lessons as well as the constant use of the environment.

Before 1978 two well-known Geography teachers, Olive Garnett and Eric Barker, were more concerned with teaching skills in Geography than in formulating schemes for 7 to 9-year-olds. Both were very concerned about the teaching of map skills and Eric Barker presumed that content would be Britain and the World. Neither put as much emphasis on the use of the environment as geographers have done during the 1970s. Both approved integration, with some reservations. Olive Garnett took for granted that the integration would be with Time, and called these two disciplines 'the obverse and reverse of the same coin'.[7] She also hoped that a trained geographer would be able to advise in this difficult task in each school. Eric Barker also presumed that the integration would be with Time but that in such blending Place lost much of its educational value.[8] Perhaps in the future we should think more about an integration of Place, Mathematics and Science. Barker rightly thought that a scheme based on skills and concepts rather than content was very difficult to plan and teach. Olive Garnett, as many post-Plowden teachers, viewed Place before the age of 8 as 'not Geography' and as a series of topics chosen by children (e.g., animals, weather, vehicles, a farm, measuring).

Between 1978 and 1982 a number of important contributions has been made to the question of content, and several new series of textbooks have given examples of how these ideas can be carried out. Perhaps the most thorough has been the Geographical Association handbook already mentioned, *Geographical Work in Primary and Middle Schools* edited by David Mills, with contributions from specialists in different fields. The 1981 edition lays greater emphasis on younger children than the previous publication. This volume is more of a staff-room reference book and covers much more than the 5 to 9 age-range. A less expensive and bulky publication is *The Study of Places in the Primary School*, one of the ILEA curriculum guidelines (1981). As mentioned in Chapter 1, it is excellently presented and illustrated and spends much time on the 5 to 9 age-range, emphasising the need for continuity (and therefore a school scheme) in these years as well as later. A matrix giving examples of direct and indirect experiences and graphicacy (the understanding and use of maps) is clearly set out but a non-specialist needs advice from a geographer to use it effectively.

Avon LEA, as already mentioned, has produced a joint History/Geography booklet. Part I advocates the concentric approach of considering three environmental factors from the age of 5; the local area, visits to more distant places on field work, and the study of still more distant places in books and through pictures, filmstrips, slides and films. It gives examples of second year infants studying India as a topic, first year juniors studying Australia or Canada and second year juniors studying village life in tropical Africa, Nigeria, Jamaica or the West Indies. In the particular scheme worked out in one school, Place and Time are interrelated (taught alongside each other and related in content) but not integrated. This booklet has the advantage of being cheap, concerned with both Place and Time and a suggested framework rather than a blueprint, and so allowing for the individual needs of schools. The new trends in teaching about Place in the 5 to 9 age-range, as with upper juniors, have changed from absolute reliance on textbook and teacher's word, as also an attempt to study too many regions of the world, to an emphasis on the specific human and physical elements of the New Geography. This has led to insistence on field work and environmental study even for the youngest children, to strong links with Mathematics in measuring and mapwork, and to a new type of highly pictorial textbook. These books demand active learning from their readers, by setting specific tasks to be undertaken.

Looking at the new textbook series we may gain some insight into framework or content suitable for children aged 7 to 9. A useful analysis is to be found in a recent article in which four new series are compared with three established ones.[9] The differences between the texts lie in greater emphasis being placed in the new ones on mathematical, scientific and historical, as well as verbal, skills. The new texts also use more environmental topics than the older, seeming to repeat topics in the 7 to 9 age-range, but in fact developing them and using them in more advanced ways. The new books also give case studies of topics already studied from a wider world. Thus they expect a wider range of topics to be studied, and at the same time use more detailed local work and field visits. In all ways more is expected of children studying Place by the time they are 9 years old.

The most definitive of the few concrete suggestions from specialists

Figure 2.5: Geographical Work for 7-9s

Some Key Ideas	Some Geographical Topics/Themes	Some General Themes	Some Particular Activities
Physical studies Weather varies during each month and year	Weather studies	Weather studies	Observation and recording of temperature, rainfall, clouds Use compass directions
Landscapes vary (valleys, hills, mountains)	Simple landscapes/river studies	Mountains, Rivers	Observation and recording Study pictures Make models and maps
Rocks and soils vary	Simple rock and soil studies	Rocks and Buildings The Sea Shore Soils and Land Use	Collecting Experimenting with rocks — hard, soft, colour, texture Simple classification Introduction to sampling
Local environment Buildings are of different ages and used for different functions	Houses, Streets, Shops	Local Environment	Observation and recording Classification Use local 1:10 000 maps, make own map Simple house, street models
Shops provide different goods, shops are grouped			

Figure 2.5 (Continued)

Some Key Ideas	Some Geographical Topics/Themes	Some General Themes	Some Particular Activities
Distant areas Farms vary in type	Farm Studies	On the Farm Food	Make plans of farms Case studies (visit farm)
Areas of world have different climates	Climates of different areas of world	The Cold Lands The Hot Lands	Study pictures, readings
Animals/people adapt to different environments	Area Studies	Africa, Australia	Study world and continental maps Models Collage Graphs

Key Resources
1:2,500, 1:10,000 OS maps of local area
Wall map of world, Globe
Weather instruments

Summary
By the end of the second year in the primary school the pupils should have:
1. undertaken field work in local area using appropriate recording techniques;
2. completed a log of weather changes;
3. made use of globe and local maps;
4. undertaken some simple landscape studies;
5. studied some environments different from their own area.

Source: D. Mills (ed.) Geographical work in Primary and Middle Schools (Geographical Association, 1981), p. 14.

comes from the David Mills' Geographical Association book and this scheme can be clarified even more specifically for non-specialists in Figure 2.5. Thus every year, physical, local and distant areas should be studied in increasing difficulty. Each school should make a scheme to avoid repetition of topics. The chart in Figure 2.6 is my framework to suggest areas of work to be included, in varying amounts in different

Figure 2.6: Separate Place Studies for 7-9s
(4-6 topics should be chosen)

	Term 1	Term 2	Term 3
Physical studies	Weather studies Mountains/rivers Rocks, Buildings, Seashore		
Local environment			Houses, streets, shops, local environment study, field work
Distant lands		Animals, food, clothes, cold lands, hot lands (Africa, Australia)	

schools. Weather studies could be an ongoing exercise started in the first term of the 7 to 8 year, if not earlier, and continued throughout the two years by the children, without much help from the teacher. I have suggested that the local work should be done in the summer term because of the need for better weather for field visits, though the Autumn Term is often a less congested time of year from the point of view of the general public. Distant lands are studied more vicariously through books, videotapes and television programmes, so this work could be done during the second term in the less good weather. The teachers concerned must be left to select specific local areas and distant lands, according to their locality, interests and other resources.

If this scheme is adopted, two textbooks might be used to provide appropriate reading and visual matter. Some children prefer to work 'through' a textbook and the average and less average learn more this way. The able flourish on using the scheme as suggested and selecting relevant material from several books to build up their own notebooks. Let us imagine that a junior school, or first school, has selected these topics (Figure 2.7) from our chart for work done on Place in the first two years:

Figure 2.7: Topics on Place

Terms	1	2	3
Age 7-8	Weather Studies The Seashore	Animals Africa	Houses, streets, shops
Age 8-9	Mountains/rivers	Cold lands	Environmental study of an urban area

Using two books the following work can be done. From Gordon Elliott's *Oxford New Geography*[10] these pages should be used:

Weather Studies	Book 2, Unit 4, pp. 26-34
Animals	Book 1, Unit 1, p. 4
	Unit 6, pp. 56-66
Houses, streets, shops	Book 1, Unit 3, p. 26
	Unit 5, p. 48
	Unit 7, pp. 68, 70, 72
	Book 2, Unit 1, pp. 2-10
	Unit 3, pp. 18-26
	Unit 8, pp. 58-66
Mountains/rivers	Book 2, Unit 11, pp. 74-82
Cold lands	Book 2, Unit 12, pp. 86-7

Malcolm Renwick and Bill Pick's *Going Places*, Book 1[11] would also help with Shops and Shopping, Families and Homes and Roads. The two omissions from our scheme are Africa and the environmental study, which cannot be provided by a textbook. Thus the teacher would have to find her own basic material on these two topics from other textbooks and reading books. Therefore one either follows a good textbook as your guidelines, or formulates one's own scheme and buys the books most in keeping with it. But in writing of the ILEA matrix, David Mills says 'local environmental work should be a recurring activity throughout the primary school' (p. 167). In all these schemes the teacher must view the topics as a beginning to studying themes that are local, national and taken from as many lands as possible, according to resources. She must also constantly use globe and atlas as a unifying factor for the scheme. The middle double-page spread of the Place notebook should be a sketch-map (duplicated) with a build-up of all the places studied on it (continents, rivers, mountains, towns, countries, routes).

Schemes for Time as a Separate Area of the Curriculum in the 7 to 9 Age-range

Emphasis on maps for Place is complemented by emphasis on sequence/time-lines for Time. This is the unifying factor for Time. All topics studied, whether chronology is favoured or not in the scheme, must be constantly related to a sequence/time-line.

During the last twenty years teachers have been encouraged to change their schemes and ways of teaching Time rather too frequently to engender confidence and enable them to build up expertise and resources. Peter Sudworth takes the reader through the changes, starting from the formal chronological approach, known by John West as 'utter end through the ages'.[12] This would allocate early History of the Stone Ages, Ancient Britons, Romans, Saxons up to 1066 to the first year junior stage (age 7-8) and the heart of the Middle Ages up to 1500 to the second year (age 8-9). The 1967 Plowden Report agreed with a more flexible approach and teachers tended to let children 'discover' the past. Some children found discovery difficult with minimal help, and became confused as to what topics to choose, not knowing the availability of resources or the extent of their teachers' knowledge. During this 1967 to 1978 period, some schools continued the chronological approach, while others developed 'topic' approaches,[13] basing their work on projects, at times purely historical but more often integrated. Many based their schemes on excellent radio and television programmes, and yet still others developed scholarly and thorough local environmental schemes, using local resources and structured field work near home and also away from their own areas. This depended very much on the desire of the head teacher, as away visits required much financial support and administrative organisation. It is to be feared that some schools abandoned Time studies altogether, as too difficult to prepare and execute with inadequate resources. In other words, the years 1967 to 1978 and even beyond, threw up a great variety of approaches. Nor was there much help from in-service courses, advisers or HMI. Up to 1978, little thought was given to the 5 to 7 age-range in relation to Time.

The 1978 HMI Report emphasised the need for a 'framework' but left each school to work out its own scheme. Little actual help was given by this Report and only certain very interested LEAs with History Advisers have been able to generate enough energy to formulate 'guidelines'. In most cases these have been typed for the internal use of their own schools but in a few cases they have been published and made generally available. The ILEA and Avon, already mentioned, are two of such authorities. In addition to LEAs, individual teachers and lecturers have discussed and formulated schemes for the primary school, trying to provide a real 'framework' flexible enough to allow each school to plan its own scheme, yet firm enough to give confidence. It is to be hoped that this will give continuity when pupils transfer from first to middle, or primary to high schools. So far the most articulate and helpful comes from a primary headmaster, Paul Noble, who also wrote a hard-hitting and honest article on the need for more specific guidelines.[14] In this he says that even those LEAs which have produced guidelines frequently 'fudge the question of content' as they fear the criticism of being too rigid. But he also sees the danger of rigidity when he writes, 'We need guidelines, not tramlines.' In his pamphlet he favours the keeping of 'subjects' in primary schools as long as they do not become 'subject barriers'. He believes that all primary schools in one area should have certain common elements in their schemes so that they can co-operate when possible and avoid the overuse of local facilities, such as museums and country houses, at the same time of year. This would necessitate the help of an LEA Adviser to co-ordinate the area. Use of local resources is essential in primary schools since all young children need first-hand experience, plenty of training in observation and the use of concrete and tangible evidence, in order to stimulate their imaginations. He is specific about timing for historical material and suggests one to one-and-a-half hours each week for the 7 to 9 age-group, increasing in the last two years of primary schooling. The flexibility of his scheme allows for what he calls 'the happy accident' of, for example, one primary school being involved in the excavation of a Roman villa in its own grounds. Such an opportunity should provide an excellent deviation from any scheme and this is easier if the scheme is reasonably flexible. For his own school Paul Noble uses the framework shown in Figure 2.8. In all cases Paul Noble suggests using as many local examples and visits as an area allows. Although this framework has been initiated for a particular school, it could easily be adapted to most schools.[15]

As in the case of Place, junior textbooks have tended to set the

Figure 2.8: Paul Noble's Framework

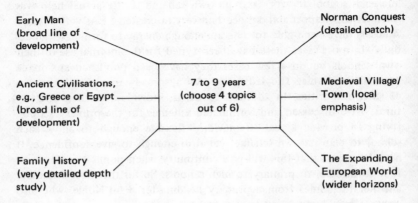

pattern for frameworks, and, since 1978 several new series have been published. Are these texts a real breakthrough as in the case of the *Outset Geography* series by S. Catling, T. Firth and D. Rowbotham (Oliver and Boyd, 1981)? Are they still the chronological race through Time? A topic approach often retains chronology by concentrating in depth on certain themes in chronological sequence. Is this the same old framework, a 'wolf in sheep's clothing'?

The three published series I shall consider all presume that 7 to 8-year-olds do not study the past. Be that as it may, much of the material from the first two books of each series could easily be adapted to the 7 to 9 age-range, especially as primary teachers have been told repeatedly in recent years that they underestimate the intelligence and ability of their charges. *History First* edited by Tom Corfe (CUP, 1976 onwards) is a series of nine units of work from world history, planned chronologically from Cassivellaunus to Queen Victoria. Each unit consists of three small booklets for children to read, twelve workcards, a set of spirit duplicator masters, a large wall picture and teachers' notes. Although still chronological, this series provides activity through the workcards, duplicated sheets, short books to read and a visual approach through the wall picture and the great number of illustrations. *Oxford Junior History* (OUP, 1980) also adopts the chronological approach, the first two books being *The Invaders* and *The Middle Ages*. This series is concerned with British History, but the new element is the link with the BBC programmes *History Long Ago* and *History Not So Long Ago*. These two new series are still relying on the mainly British history chronological approach, though the illustrations and methods teachers are encouraged to use have a 'new look'. As the books are selling well, it appears that primary teachers still want to plan their content on a chronological basis. Is this through fear of the new, or educational conviction? In many cases it is honestly believed that a chronological syllabus will help to teach time-sense. Yet John West has proved conclusively in his research in Dudley schools that a non-chronological framework taught with constant reference to sequence/time-lines is more effective in teaching historical time.[16]

A third recent series breaks new ground from the point of view of chronology. This is *History Around You* edited by Allan Waplington and published by Oliver and Boyd (1981) and again intended for children of 8 years old and over. This is linked closely with the Granada TV series *History Around You* and owes much to the thought of the *Schools Council Project 8-13, Place, Time and Society*. Although there is an elaborate and colourful time-line from the Romans to Elizabeth II the approach is concentric. The History children have 'around' them (i.e., local history) is used as evidence or 'clues' to the past and the first two books are concerned with the child's home environment and his immediate village/suburb/town environment. The books are profusely illustrated with 'clues' for children to use as evidence.

Two out of three of these series are dependent upon television programmes which all schools cannot watch or videotape. A fourth series which may be published in the future is that thought out by Alistair Ross, a practising primary teacher and trained historian. It is based on five approaches to the past and could be used either as a separate History scheme or as part of an integrated one. The five approaches are a period or patch of History (e.g., The Victorians, The 1930s), a line of development (e.g., Farming), a personality (e.g., Boudicca), an event of importance (e.g., the Peasants' Revolt) and local/family history (e.g., a family biography). Each approach is studied in each of four books as a complete unit with no chronological relationship with other units in the book. Thus 7-year-olds would study the 1950s, the Home, Mrs Milburn in The Second World War, 1066 and My Family. In the belief that John West's advocacy of a non-chronological approach with the constant use of time-lines is correct, this series would provide time-lines in all books. Thus 7-year-olds would learn to move freely on their time-line from the 1950s to, possibly, Stone Age Homes, to the Second World War, back to 1066 and finally to their own twentieth-century family and home. At the same time a class need not study all these topics in one year; the Home could easily be used with work in Place (Andy's Home in *Outset Geography I* would complement it well). It seems, therefore, that Alistair Ross' scheme would provide study in depth, as well as four approaches which could be used in a separate or integrated syllabus. It could also be used in a traditional chronological syllabus if all four books were bought and used between classes. This is quite new, and like the concentric approach of *History Around You* adopts a non-chronological philosophy to thinking about the past. Nor is it dependent upon a television programme. It has the additional advantages of providing a broader historical perspective than the purely local one, encouraging the use of real historical evidence of greater variety than 'the near at hand'. Therefore of the two 'breakthroughs' in textbook series, that proposed by Alistair Ross probably provides the children with a more enriching experience.[17]

So far I have considered recent trends in schemes for Time for the 7 to 9 age-range since 1978, using LEA guidelines, enthusiastic individual teachers and textbooks. A fourth source of inspiration is that of Dr Marjorie Reeves in her method book to accompany the 'Then and There' series (Longman, 1956 onwards). This book is called *Why History?* (1980) but is also concerned with how to teach Time to younger children. Although the 'Then and There' series is too difficult for 5 to 9-year-olds these patch approach booklets are full of up-to-date scholarship and new ideas for all teachers of Time. Chapter 8 is concerned with 'Planning Syllabuses: some suggestions'. Dr Reeves writes 'So I suggest that Patches and Threads should form the pattern of our syllabus making',[18] some recurring in different forms at later stages. This last idea is an echo of Bruner's 'spiral curriculum', and in keeping with Allan Waplington's 'concentric approach' in *History Around You*. Her suggestions for the first two junior years (7-9) are given in Figure 2.9. As in Paul Noble's scheme, selection would be made to suit individual pupils and teachers. Most of these frameworks put forward since 1978 favour choice of topics, study of a variety of periods from ancient times to the contemporary world and the constant use of time-lines to develop chronology.

So where do we stand in 1983? Is there a consensus of opinion to abandon chronology and not attempt to cover too much ground superficially, and in a boring, generalised way? There is not much consensus, but we should be edging towards something more sophisticated and scholarly than what has passed for History (if done at all) in most primary schools. In Figure 2.10 I put forward two alternative suggestions for the 7 to 9 age-range.

Figure 2.9: Time Scheme for 7-9s: Marjorie Reeves

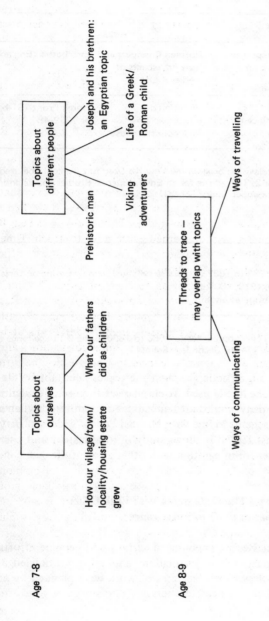

Source: Marjorie Reeves, *Why History?* (Longman, 1980) (adapted)

Figure 2.10: History Syllabuses
A

Terms	1	2	3
Age 7-8	Roman Empire and Roman Britain	Norman Conquest and Rule *or* Aspects of Medieval Life	Elizabethan England
Age 8-9	Civil War in the seventeenth century Local visit	Victorian *or* Edwardian Life Visit country house	Home Front 1914-18 *or* 1939-45

Note: The Yorkshire television programme *How We Used to Live* could be used in the last term of year 2. This allows for an Environmental Studies course and/or World History in the upper Junior School.

B

7-9 (All terms)

Family History from 1983 to 1837 (regressive syllabus), concentrating on certain dates e.g., 1950, 1940, 1910, 1857 etc.
Plenty of museum visits are essential

Note: This allows for Topic approaches to 1066 to 1800 in the 9-11 age-range and Aspects of World History in the Secondary School.

Syllabus A is more didactic although the topics need not be taught in this order if a time-line is used. It emphasises the use of evidence in depth studies, so many important happenings are omitted. Syllabus B is a Social History scheme in line with Michael Pollard's ideas in *History with Juniors* (Evans, 1973). It allows study of local history and visits as well as opportunities for integration with other areas of the curriculum.

Schemes for Place and Time Integrated with Each Other and Other Disciplines in the 7 to 9 Age-range

The 1967 Plowden Report encouraged serious and genuine efforts to integrate the primary school curriculum and present knowledge to children as a 'seamless robe'. Schemes of work were planned by able, knowledgeable and experienced teachers and in many cases good efforts were made to carry these out with the help of increased resources and the support of teachers' centres staffed by Advisory teachers. Many LEAs ran suitable in-service courses to help teachers. Those situated in areas of historic and geographical renown encouraged schools to adopt a strongly environmental approach. With such help these integrated courses were usually successful but in those less well-endowed areas of the country this approach was found too difficult and either no Place or Time were studied, or recourse was had to a shallow chronological course for Time, and a purely regional course for Place. Ideally, these integrated schemes involved many disciplines but in fact they often resulted in the combination of Place and Time to form Environmental Studies.

The pros and cons of integration have led to much argument among educationalists but it is recommended that Place and Time are integrated or interrelated at some stage in the 7 to 11 years of schooling. In 1965 Moray House College of Education, Edinburgh, advocated that 8 to 9-year-olds should study 'the school in its environment: links with other disciplines'.[19] Two years later the Chief HMI for Primary Education, John Blackie, also suggested for the 8 to 9 age-range 'History integrated with Geography'.[20] The great advantage of integration is that children have more chance to see the relationship between different parts of the curriculum and to learn to think more broadly and thematically than in subject areas. So teachers would start with a topic or centre of interest such as 'Discovery' or 'Warfare' and lead their class into many concepts basic to Place and Time. These are huge and at times sophisticated areas which could be handled magnificently or very inadequately. Another advantage is the very large number and variety of resources needed to be consulted which extends the need for children to find and consult a wider spectrum of information than does a single subject. It could also involve team teaching, in which case children would benefit from the expertise of more than one teacher, possibly exchanging classes in one year. Lastly, an integrated topic can be pursued over longer periods, and more frequently. This leads to uninterrupted work with more resources for whole afternoons and encourages well-prepared and followed-up visits outside school. Thus the philosophy and reasoning behind integrated topics is sound and can work if planned in detail and well-resourced.

Arguments against integration are also persuasive. The knowledge required by the teacher is phenomenal at any but a superficial standard. In addition using this knowledge to integrate is a very difficult task, involving intellectual and practical abilities. The collection of appropriate, wide-ranging resources and the maintenance of these resources in working order is also required. Another argument against integration is the lack of balance in subject areas on a given theme and the temptation for teachers to 'drag in' as many 'subjects' as possible, often in an artificial way, for the sake of appearances. Thus any Environnental Studies syllabus is very frequently found to be dominated by Geography and Science at the expense of History. The children can also suffer if the topic is too wide-ranging, for they may have too much scope for dilettante learning, so becoming confused by a loose-knit, rather vague treatment resulting in little solid learning.

Whether one adopts integration or single subject schemes, the whole span of school life has to be considered. Any scheme for the 7 to 9 age-range depends upon what is done in the 5 to 7 and 9 to 11 age-ranges. Most teachers of infants find Place and Time come naturally into an integrated curriculum, but differences of opinion arise over older juniors. Decisions depend upon the particular school, children, teachers and environment (the 'four variables' of the *Schools Council Project 8-13, Place, Time and Society*).[21] Teachers may have to adopt the scheme required by the school to give variety of approach to pupils and avoid repetition of topics. Repetition is permissable if a real effort is made to show that a more detailed developmental scheme is used on the same topic later on in schooling. Obviously, separate subject teaching might develop a topic touched on in an earlier integrated scheme, or vice versa. For example, 7-year-olds studying Roman Britain in their first term and using local examples if they lived near Hadrian's Wall or Cirencester, might use some of the knowledge in their fourth year in an Environmental Studies scheme on 'Roads' or 'Fortifications'. If this is known by all teachers then reference can be made to later or earlier work, and care taken not to repeat exact information but to use it in another context. This type of treatment is very valuable but it must be planned.

Having already considered suggestions for separate Place and Time schemes earlier in this chapter I shall put forward several integrated ones and then offer my own suggestions. The first suggestions come from Schools Council Projects. In Chapter 1 of this book the *Environmental Studies Project 5-13* was discussed. This mainly took good examples from schools and emphasised the Place element of Environmental Studies, but did not suggest any particular schemes. The same applied to *Place, Time and Society* which put emphasis on the need for teachers to work out their own schemes on the basis of the skills, concepts and objectives given by it. Some teachers found this too time-consuming or daunting and these ideas have not been taken up system-atically, although some LEAs, notably ILEA and Merton, favoured them. More recently the first Director of the project, Professor Alan Blyth of the University of Liverpool, adapted the ideas to the 7 to 11 age-range.[22] In this scheme he catered for both separate Time teaching and 'interrelated social studies'. In the latter, children of 7 to 8 would study 'Signs, Messages and Stories'. This would start with the develop-ment of language (including how animals talk and the beginnings of writing and the various alphabets) and continue with 'Stories and Storytellers' (through the Ages) and 'Messages' (objects, photographs, museum treasures, festivals, rituals). 8 to 9-year-olds would study 'Simple Societies', involving hunters, farmers, inventors and traders. It would be possible to select four interrelated topics from these sugges-tions and use them during the two years as a scheme of work. They all involve all societies of the world and do not emphasise particular per-sonalities or places of importance. They are simply a loose framework expecting teachers to use much initiative in a detailed scheme.

As this Schools Council scheme is biased towards Social Studies, the more usual Environmental Studies schemes are biased towards local Place and Time. If Environmental Studies is covered in the early years of the Junior School extensive field visits are more difficult to execute with safety, but local day and half-day visits are possible, particularly in the 8 to 9 age-range. In an Historical Association pamphlet Dr P.J. Rogers of the Queen's University, Belfast, reasons that local concrete evidence is the easiest for young children to handle, and since evidence is essential for a study of Time 'there would seem to be a strong case for commencing with local studies and working through these towards matters of more general significance.'[23] Dr Rogers, for one, would start with Environmental Studies in the 7 to 9 age-range. Following up his idea I suggest that a scheme could be built up around specific and well-prepared local visits, two in the first year and three in the second. These might include a walk round the environs of their own school, visits to a nearby village/town[24], a farm, a local museum and a country house. Preparation and follow-up would take the class-time for these visits. An example of a visit to a country house, Croxteth Hall, near Liverpool, is given in full for 6-year-olds in Chapter 6 and could easily be adapted for 7 to 9-year-olds.

The Avon LEA scheme, already discussed in the Place section of this chapter (see p. 19), may be used as an interrelated scheme as well as a separate Place/Time one, which makes it a most adaptable framework. This scheme (Figure 2.11) has the additional advantage of suggesting

Figure 2.11: History/Geography Syllabus: 7-9s

	Autumn Term	Spring Term	Summer Term	Development of Basic, Graphical and Historical Skills
Year 1	Midsomer Norton and Radstock district, today and in the documents etc. Traffic studies Discussion on future development, parks, homes for elderly, industry, shops, leisure centres etc. Litter detection	The Romans (a) in Britain: remains, Boudicca, Caractacus (b) Empire: soldiers, gods, clothes, life-style	A place in the 'old' Commonwealth, e.g. Australia or Canada	Language work Number work Vocabulary extension (a checklist at end of each term to show words introduced) Concept of space, making maps and plans Use of local maps Putting information on maps Use of atlases and globes, when relevant

Figure 2.11 (Continued)

	Autumn Term	Spring Term	Summer Term	Development of Basic, Graphical and Historical Skills
	A neighbouring city, Bath Places of interest, where they are and how to get there	The Georgians Georgian Bath: architecture, fashion, Beau	A developing place with links with Britain, e.g., Nigeria or Jamaica or West Indies as a whole	Lessons in map reading, direction, symbols, measuring, empathy
Year 2	Industry, tourism, the arts etc. Use of large and small-scale maps	Nash, the season, Nelson, Wellington, Napoleon, Aspects of the Slave Trade, French Revolution, American Independence, Industrial Revolution (beginnings)		Concept of time, chronology and sequencing types of evidence, written, primary, secondary, pictorial, photographic Recording and organising information, empathy

Source: *History and Geography in the Primary School* (Avon LEA, 1982), p. 16

the basic geographical and historical skills to be taught (as in the 5 to 7 scheme in Figure 2.3).

Links between Place and Time are the most usual but Time has been linked with Science in various ways. The first attempt to do this was in the *Nuffield Junior Science Project* mentioned in Chapter 1. In this, 7-year-olds studied 'Cavemen' referring to making fire, cavemen's clothes, stone tools, vegetable dyes, pottery and cave-paintings. The activities were mainly concerned with experimentation, in truly scientific fashion. Voyages of discovery, and transport could be studied in the same way, linking with Science.[25] The *Schools Council Science Project 5-13* related Time to Science through time measurement, biological clocks and people and time. A display of old clocks led to many activities such as King Alfred's candle clock, shadow clocks in the playground, Big Ben, a graph on the bedtime of children and the artist's use of clocks.[26] From these examples it is clear that Science is the central theme and the other elements are 'invited in' when appropriate. This tends to encourage bits of information, and to require much erudition from teachers.

More recent than either of these projects is a book by Peter Prosser showing how Science, Place and Time can be integrated. It is called *The World on Your Doorstep* (McGraw-Hill, 1982). Although no actual syllabus is given and the book applies to children aged 7 to 13, Peter Prosser shows in detail, using diagrams, photographs and flow-charts, how certain topics may be studied in depth, such as 'Walls and Hedges', 'Flint' (an integrated topic) and 'The Churchyard'. In all these themes he shows how Science, Place and Time can be successfully integrated. This approach shows how 'discovery learning' can be tackled in detail. It is a 'new look' at the old Plowden integrated themes.

An ambitious integrated scheme for Topic time has been started at Grove Junior School, Birmingham, which has a multi-cultural intake. It involves nine subject areas and is used by the whole school. Place and Time appear for two-ninths of the time as separate subjects and are used by other disciplines in the remaining seven-ninths. This applies to all subjects. In the first year of the junior school (7-8) prehistory is studied, including a visit to the local museum. There are links with Religious Education in 'Sun-worship', with Place in 'Use of the Globe' and with Science in 'Animals and Water Creatures'. 8 to 9-year-olds study human society in simple agricultural communities, introducing specific examples such as Red Indians and Bedouins, for example. The later junior years are concerned with the development of society up to the present time. This Grove scheme may seem somewhat ambitious unless teachers know exactly how to prepare their work and are given help (and time!) with reading and appropriate resources. The aim of introducing children to the development of society culminating in their own is worthy, though care would have to be taken to introduce inte-resting personalities at sensible points.[27]

The integration of Music, Dance and Drama with Time is a more specialised activity, appropriate only at certain stages in the 7 to 9 age-range. Most junior schools encourage singing, recorder playing and the playing of other more sophisticated musical instruments. *This Merry Company* by Alison and Michael Bagenal[28] offers most construct-ive advice to teachers on medieval dance, medieval plays with musical accompaniment and the making of medieval musical instruments. Oxford University Press has published two books (teachers and pupils), a cassette of music for the plays, and spoken instructions for learning the improvised medieval dances. The first play, *Chanticleer and Pertelote* (taken from Chaucer's *Canterbury Tales*)[29] is a farmyard drama involving children impersonating animals, and is the most suitable for younger juniors. Detailed instructions encourage children to discuss the tale as the Canterbury pilgrims did, and there are enough characters to occupy a whole class. This work would be suitable for a half or whole term's work in the right setting, and is a depth study of one part of medieval life (1250-1400). It could be linked to a study of Chaucer's *Canterbury Tales* and his pilgrims, so introducing a literary element into the integration.

Place and Time can be integrated with many areas of the curriculum, particularly with the creative arts and mathematics. But they also seem to integrate with each other naturally, especially in any local study. But whether the scheme of work is an integrated one or separate subjects, content does matter and a framework should be decided and honoured in every school.

Notes

1. *Education 5 to 9: an Illustrative Survey of 80 First Schools in England* (HMSO, 1982) p. 59.
2. D. Mills (ed.), *Geographical Work in Primary and Middle Schools* (Geo-graphical Association, 1981).
3. J.E. Blyth, *History in Primary Schools* (McGraw-Hill, 1982) pp. 22-9.
4. Family History Patches (Nelson) include *The Stonors*, *The Steels*, *The Lloyds* and *The Logans*.
5. *History and Geography in Primary Schools* (Avon LEA, 1982).
6. J. Dewey, *Experience and Education* (Collier Books, 1976) p. 78.

7. O. Garnett, *Fundamentals of School Geography* (Harrap, 1951) p. 317.

8. E.J. Barker, *The Junior Geography Lesson* (OUP, 1968) and *Geography and Younger Children* (OUP, 1974).

9. A. Turner and S. Catling. 'A New Consensus in Primary Geography', *Teaching Geography* vol. 8, no. 1, (July 1982).

10. G. Elliott, *Oxford New Geography* (OUP, 1980).

11. M. Renwick and B. Pick, *Going Places* (Nelson, 1979).

12. P. Sudworth 'An Analysis of History Teaching in the Primary School since 1960', *Teaching History* no. 33, (June 1982).

13. A. and R. Earl, *How Shall I Teach History?* (Blackwell, 1971).

14. P. Noble, *Time-Sense* (privately published, 1981) available from the author, April Cottage, 40 High St., Broad Blundsden, Swindon, Wilts. 'Primary History: What Guidelines are needed?', *Teaching History*, no. 33, (June 1982).

15. P. Noble's ideas are given in detail in a forthcoming pamphlet: A. Low-Beer and J.E. Blyth, *Teaching History to Younger Children* (Historical Association, T.H. 52, 1983).

16. J. West and J. Lally, *The Child's Awareness of the Past*, Teachers' Guidelines (Hereford and Worcester County Council, 1981).

17. This series is under consideration by a publishing house.

18. M. Reeves, *Why History?* (Longman, 1980), p. 77.

19. *History in the Primary School: a Scheme of Work* (Moray House College of Education, 1965).

20. J.B. Blackie, *Inside the Primary Classroom* (HMSO, 1967).

21. W.A.L. Blyth *et al.*, *Place, Time and Society 8-13: Curriculum Planning in History, Geography and Social Science* (Collins/ESL, 1976), p. 13.

22. J.E. Blyth, *Primary Schools*, Figures 3.15 to 3.18, pp. 56-9.

23. P.J. Rogers, *The New History: theory into practice* (Historical Association, T.H. 44, 1979), p. 25.

24. S. Scoffham, *Using the School's Surroundings: A Guide to Local Studies in Urban Schools* (Ward Lock, 1980).

25. *Science and History*, Teaching Background Booklet, Nuffield Junior Science (Collins, 1967).

26. *Time* (Macdonald, 1969) gives a flow chart for display of old clocks.

27. More details are given in Low-Beer and Blyth.

28. A. and H. Bagenal, *This Merry Company* (OUP, 1979).

29. Ian Serraillier, *The Road to Canterbury* (Heinemann, 1981) is a useful reference book for teachers.

Part Two

PRACTICE IN THE CLASSROOM

3 METHODS OF APPROACH

Young children are more influenced by *how* information is taught than *what* information is taught. Place and Time are both 'information' subjects and both require certain common skills for children to learn. Therefore I am considering methods of approach in three parts. The first looks at the approaches which are common to both Place and Time. The similarity in the disciplines makes this part the most detailed. The second will consider approaches specific to Place, in which graphicacy holds a large place. The last part is approaches specific to Time, in this case much concerned with sequence/time-lines and time charts. In the last two parts much material is given which helps both Place and Time. In all three parts, the whole age-range of 5 to 9 will be considered.

Approaches Common to Place and Time

Information-type areas of the curriculum, such as Place and Time, have common problems for young children since their memories are not very retentive yet the skills specific to such areas require certain basic knowledge for them to be practised. I shall subdivide this part of the chapter into those common approaches which are much used, are basic to the disciplines and can be applied without too many extra resources, and those used more irregularly.

The basic approaches are:

1. Teacher-initiated oral work starting from story-telling and developing into questionning and class discussion or 'talking with children', in the words of Joan Tough[1]
2. The use of illustrations of all types
3. The use of books
4. Written work and the keeping of records by children
5. Field work and all forms of going out of school and visits, including museum visits
6. The practice of Place and Time vocabulary

I have put these six approaches in the order in which most teachers use them in the 5 to 9 age-range. For example, until children can write, the third and fourth are not much used and visits usually take place in the summer term, when preparation has been made through discussion, looking at books and reading them. Field work also involves recording, at least on return to school if not 'on site' and this has to be learnt by 5 to 9-year-olds.

Teacher-initiated Oral Work

The popularity of 'discovery learning' has tended to lessen the need for teachers to give children information by talking to them. At the same time the telling, or even reading, of stories has fallen into disuse. The traditional use of story-time at the end of the day in the infant school has tended to be looked upon as a relaxation from the serious work of number, language, creative work and physical education. This is a pity, as this medium is the only effective one in the very early years of schooling for teaching Place and Time, and could be used at any time in the school day. In her comments on the HMI Report on first schools (*Education 5 to 9: an Illustrated Survey of 80 First Schools in England*, HMSO, 1982) Rosemary Clayfield, of London University Institute of Education, criticises the report for not emphasising the need for story-telling as an integral part of the day's work, yet praises the Report for the importance it attaches to 'developing talking and listening skills'.[2]

The method of telling a good story is common to Place and Time and, for that matter, to all story-telling:

1. Read the story twice from its original source, visualising people and actions (more necessary for Time than Place).
2. Plan the story in four to six parts and give a title to each part.
3. Put exact words to each character involved in the story and write them down for easy reference.
4. Try to see the action of the story happening in your preparation before you tell it (children often visualise the story better by closing their eyes, which also avoids too many distractions).

This should be followed by prepared questions initiating discussion with the class.[3] It could also lead to role-playing and written work after a series of stories for 8 to 9-year-old children. Most stories are made more real by the use of large illustrations which are preferable to a whole class straining to see small pictures in the story book. A more detailed discussion with examples of story-telling in Time is in a book I wrote some years ago.[4] The ILEA pamphlet[5] has a full list of suitable story books for Place arranged according to difficulty, with books for younger juniors first in the sections concerned with different parts of the world. As whole books, these would form half a term's or a term's work, on say, Australasia or Africa, if used in their entirety. Alternatively, the teacher would need to select certain key chapters. Both Place and Time stories are concerned with *difference*. Place stories introduce children to different people in different places today. Time stories introduce them to different people at different times in the past and sometimes in different places. Story-telling is the most effective way to show children how different they are from other people and ages, which broadens their experience and should help to develop a tolerant attitude.

From straight story-telling concluded by a few questions teachers can initiate good discussion lessons, particularly with the 7 to 9-year-olds, who should be better trained to listen to each other than younger children. Where question and answer and further question and answer takes place, not only are children being stimulated to think for themselves but they are being given practice and confidence in speaking in front of other people, eventually without embarassment. Teachers should be careful to prepare the leading questions to be asked and make time to vary the type of question. 'Closed' questions require a factual, information-type answer, which is usually right or wrong. One such question might be 'Through which country does the River Nile flow?', requiring the 'closed' answer 'Egypt'. Another might be 'In which year did William of Normandy invade England?' requiring the 'closed' answer '1066'. 'Open' questions, leading to critical thinking, require answers which are more a matter of opinion and are seldom right or wrong. An 'open' question might be 'Look at the map of Egypt and see how the River Nile flows into the Mediterranean Sea. How do you think the shape of this "delta" affects the Egyptians?'. The 'open' answer might be, 'It probably gives the Egyptians more trade as there are so many different openings into which foreign ships can bring their goods and take Egyptian goods away.' Another 'open' question might be 'Had William of Normandy any right to invade England?'. One answer might be 'No, he should have been content with ruling Normandy'; another might be 'Yes, Edward the Confessor had half promised him the crown of England as he had no son to succeed him.' In the case of both the Nile and 1066 it is clear that children need to be taught some facts before they are asked questions, and that answers can be right or matters of opinion. In the words of P.J. Rogers, 'the teacher is not just *in* authority but *an* authority'. Therefore teachers should only start discussions on topics which they have prepared and taught. With the age-group we are considering this type of approach is only viable when the teacher is having a class lesson. Only top juniors, trained from an early age, could have discussions in their own groups and keep to the point.

The Use of Illustrations

Although pictorial material includes maps, plans and diagrams these will be considered in more detail in the next section of this chapter, under the somewhat grandiose title, 'Graphicacy'. In this section I shall discuss how to use book illustrations, posters, large wall pictures and paintings from commercial publishers, photographs, picture postcards, slides and 'home-made' visual aids. The visual impact of the television screen will be considered in Chapter 4 as it is a highly effective and much used teaching medium.

In the introduction to his thorough and interesting pamphlet[7] Robert Unwin expresses the 1980s view that 'the visual image has largely replaced the written word as our principal means of communication'. So how much more is the illustration to be used as a teaching medium for young children who cannot read but can see, and have acute powers of observation. The most obvious picture form is that in the textbook both in Place and Time. In most modern textbook series, artists' reconstructions are supplemented by photographs, diagrams and original contemporary illustrations, in the case of Time. They are used to advantage by authors, and children are made to look carefully at the pictures by suggestions in the text. For example, in Gordon Elliott's Book 2 of the *Oxford New Geography* (suitable for 8 to 9-year-olds) in the double-page spread in 'Checking', artists' reconstructions of coal mines in 1950 and 1980 are shown and specific activities are asked of the children in relation to them.[8] Therefore teachers as well as children are led by modern authors to use the pictures. Young children who cannot yet read learn much from the careful observation of pictures in books for older juniors found in the school library. Teachers should collect such books relevant to the topic studied and also get the children to borrow them from public libraries. Questions about the pictures with page references can be put on cards and placed in a container in the front of each book and children can work on these in pairs. They can have the answer ready when the time comes for a class discussion.

Larger illustrations such as posters, Macmillan's History Class Pictures and the diagrams-cum-photographs of Pictorial Charts, as well as Museum posters, can teach incidentally by being round the classroom walls for a period of time. They can also form a visual aid at the front of the class for an oral lesson. Groups of children can gather round individual posters near which the teacher has written two or three specific questions demanding intelligent observation. Picture post-cards can be fastened onto coloured paper and supported by relevant questions and made into a small wall display for individual or group work, when a topic has been introduced. They can also be put into large envelopes with the questions on card for an individual or group to work on. Sometimes detailed postcards, such as an illuminated capital of a manuscript, need a magnifying glass to see the fine detail. Black and white photographs of different places at different times are particularly useful in the understanding of Place. Photo-analysis can be done by fastening a large clear photograph on paper and asking questions about it, with pointers to the places to find the answer in the photograph.[9]

Slides made by the school or bought from commercial firms or from the cutting up and framing of old film strips, may be used by the teacher for an oral lesson, though care should be taken not to use more than about eight to ten slides for 7 to 9-year-olds, and even fewer for infants. Children have been increasingly using small hand projectors to look at slides individually or, at most, in small groups. John West used slides in his large-scale research with children aged 7 to 11. He used slides depicting the past as documentary evidence but also as the basis for children, particularly non-readers, to construct an oral narra-tive story in their own words. He provided worksheets or cue-cards for children to use individually or in pairs in relation to particular pictures. In his excellent *Teachers' Guide* John Lally, one of John West's colla-borators, gives a list of the types of illustrations used and three examples of worksheets.[10]

'Home-made' visual aids, even if the teacher is no artist, have the merit of being absolutely relevant to the job in hand of containing the absolute essentials for that particular piece of learning. They can be made on paper or put onto the blackboard. Very often as teaching media these have more value for younger children than the more intricate commercially-produced illustrations.

The Use of Books

Something has already been said in Chapter 2 about textbooks for Place and Time. A school has to take a middle path between relying too heavily on *one* series of books which are expensive to replace in whole sets and having no basic text for the non-specialist teacher and no reading material of the right level for infants and younger juniors. Ideally, modern textbooks, even if used between two children, are an excellent basis for work if teachers can gradually build up other resources including smaller sets of reading books (six of each), packs, slides, pictures and teacher-made worksheets. Until an infant school, in collaboration with the junior school it feeds, works out a framework of Place/Time topics, there is no point in buying suitable books, though the number of publishers interested in information books for this age-range is growing. Some examples will be given in Chapter 4. Many teachers of 7 to 9 children have found the series of four books for junior schools unsuitable, as the language of the first two books is not simple enough. This has led them to believe that Place and Time, except incidentally, has no place in the 5 to 9 age-range. In 1983 more effort is being made by publishers to provide books on Place than Time. As in number and language, the textbook tends to control children's activity, and children should persevere in finding and using books regularly in this age-range. Needless to say, textbooks should be used wisely and not 'read round the class' except in dire emergencies.

In an interesting article,[11] Ralph Lavender, better known for his book *Myths, Legends and Lore* (Blackwell, 1975), gives advice on encouraging children to use information books. In the infant school, information books should be coded according to 'dipping into', 'interest' and 'identification' (the last presumably meaning 'finding out'). Young children who learn to ask questions of the text will be able to use 'relevant quotations' later on in their careers. Children should be taught how to use the contents page, index and glossary as well as the techniques of skimming and scanning both pictures and text for a particular item, or for the gist of the passage. Ralph Lavender also believes that first-hand experience (e.g., a field visit) should lead to the greater use of information books. In addition, teachers should read aloud from information books as well as fiction. It also may be necessary to provide adult books for children if their own are unsuitable. He also does not believe in any distinction being made between textbooks and reading books. This is obviously advice which applies to a whole school career, but most of it can be started in the 5 to 9 age-range.

Written Work and the Keeping of Records by Children

Children should keep some record of Place and Time from their earliest years. If an interrelated topic approach is adopted, each child should take pride in keeping a Topic Book for the year in which labelled illustrations, answers to questions, diagrams, simple maps and photographs of visits may be kept. If Place and Time are taught separately from 7 to 9 two books should be kept named Place and Time. The first should have the essential ingredients of Place, map work, clearly visible, and Time should have a simple sequence/time-line on the middle page spread to show the main framework of topics of the past studied, and their sequence, with possibly a selection of outstanding dates in the 8 to 9 age-range. Some teachers prefer to make books of coloured paper for their children, others to get the class to make concertina workbooks. Display is not enough for recording children's work, as these exhibitions are often destroyed at the end of the year, or even the term. It would be possible after a display to put certain items into individual children's books. The presentation of some brief reference to work done is most helpful to the next class teacher, if a school framework has been worked out. Continuous prose in a substantial composition can only be expected in the 8 to 9 age-range, on average, though many younger children can write a paragraph of prose if the teacher asks questions whose answers form a whole. Some schools encourage young children to tape-record their work, such as their response to a particular illustration, and keep these tapes for the school year as records.

Field Work

Children of 5 to 9 are physically active, and field work, going out of school and visits are essential and central parts of their Place/Time education. They are closely linked to map work, which will be considered in a separate section. In planning a framework, a school should first consider which places can be visited easily in a day or half a day. Margaret West, lately Infant Adviser for Wolverhampton LEA, instituted a field study centre, 'Kingswood', for infant and nursery children, to accommodate twenty children in residence and forty children for day visits.[12] Most teachers of young children are not fortunate enough to live in Wolverhampton and have to be content with half and whole day visits. It is in these local visits that the natural integration of Place and Time is made.

All the schemes suggested in Chapter 2 include local studies which involve field work/visits on however small a scale. For example, for Place, the Geographical Association suggests for 5 to 7-year-olds, local work on houses, shops, streets, traffic in streets, movement of pupils in school, local gardens, parks and open spaces and visits to 'other places in the UK'. In my own suggestion (Figure 2.4) 'Our School', 'A Farm Study' and 'The Seashore' might come in the summer term of the first infant year. An example of local emphasis and therefore the practical experience of field work in Time is Paul Noble's 7 to 9 scheme (Figure 2.8) in which his school uses as many local examples in Wiltshire as possible. Most of the textbook series also mentioned in Chapter 2 use local visits as an essential teaching approach; for example *History Around You,* linked to the Granada television series uses local evidence as clues to the past and expects children to be taken out of school. Many schools plan more visits for older juniors, especially if Environmental Studies is the planned scheme of work, but it would be a great pity if younger children had no experience of working outside school.

Whatever form field work takes, whether it is at first walking round the classroom, school and playground, as suggested by David Rowbotham,[13] or visiting a residential field centre, the visit must be planned carefully. The least amount of time for any visit is three weeks, for preparation in class, execution and follow-up. Many visits spark off longer-term activities, encompassing many areas of the curriculum and culminating in a display for parents and other classes to see, as well as the classs itself. This preparation involves a preparatory visit by the teacher, the devising of worksheets, duplicating home-made maps, providing Ordnance Survey (OS) maps on a large scale (50″ or 25″ to a mile, one between two for the 8 to 9-year-olds), as well as collecting appropriate reading books on the topic. Infants and younger juniors cannot cope with much writing on the visit and a small notebook or cluster of plain postcards are preferable to clip-boards.

Visits should concentrate on a limited number of objectives in a museum or country house intended for adults. I did this limitation in my visit to Croxteth Hall with 6-year-olds.[14] Well-run museums are a great help to teachers in providing suitable worksheets or workbooks. They are, for 5 to 9-year-olds, more controllable physically than home-made A4 worksheets. Such museums frequently employ an Education Officer experienced with younger children. Staffing ratios for visits are most important; in the 5-7 age-range one adult is needed for ten children, and in the 7 to 9 age-range, one adult for twenty children. Some teachers take portable tape-recorders on visits to record children's observations, playing them back in the classroom for discussion.

Follow-up in the classroom takes a variety of forms according to the age-range of the children concerned. Infants should be allowed to talk about their experiences as soon as possible after their visit. They should all be expected to extend it by using books, viewing slides and, above all, recording in their special notebooks some aspect of their work. They will also need help from the teacher as to how this particular visit fits into the year's scheme as a whole. It is a great stimulus to aim for a display work, involving pictorial work, models, written work, photographs and even artefacts.

Books to help teachers will be given in Chapter 4 but those who are diffident about urban field work should consult Stephen Scoffham's book, which is clearly set out and highly practical.[15] A second essential for teachers of younger juniors in incorporating Place and Time is Henry Pluckrose's *Let's Use the Locality*.[16]

The Practice of Place and Time Vocabulary

As academic disciplines, both Place and Time have a specialised vocabulary, some of which should be taught as soon as possible. The greater attention paid by geographers to the teaching of young children has focused attention on the need for teachers to 'start as they mean to go on', and publications have helped primary teachers with advice about how to approach the vocabulary problem.[17] *New Thinking in Geography* writes of the development of vocabulary use, from children talking about trees to distinguishing between types of trees, such as oaks, holly, ash etc., from vehicles to lorries, tankers and so on.[18] The seasons and weather changes can be talked of simply or geographically, involving children gaining understanding of concepts through words and more detailed concepts from more detailed terminology. The concept of Place is gained by teachers using certain words. Examples of this basic work are given by Melanie Harvey, who suggests that children should be encouraged to play games involving responding to these instructions: 'Go and stand *behind* John', 'Put the book *under* the maps' and 'Go *outside* the room'.[19] In a later section on Graphicacy we will see how Michael Storm used the words 'scale drawings' from the home to be built in *Playing with Plans*. Gradually, through the teachers' use and use in books, by the age of 9 children will use geographical terms in their talk; a river will 'meander' rather than 'go in and out'. From the age of 7 it is advisable for children to build up a specialised Place/Time vocabulary at the back of their special notebooks and refer to this list in their discussions and writing.

Time also requires the understanding of specialised terms. For example a 'century' is one hundred years and the twentieth-century has dates in the 1900s. Period names for objects such as carriage, hansom-cab, peasant, and the meaning of collective terms such as royalty, must also be taught to be understood. Jeannette Coltham's research showed that 9-year-old children confused the 'ruler' of a country with a 'ruler' on their desks and that lack of understanding of terms made learning difficult.[20] John West's research placed ongoing emphasis on historical language. In explaining this research John Lally says that it shows how the language areas of talking, listening and writing should be consistently developed during the early years of schooling. He gives five lists of words for teachers to introduce for evidence, story, time, periods, and other historical words, and suggests that they check that they are making a positive effort to introduce these words into the children's work. They should concentrate on children expressing themselves with 'precision' rather than 'generality'. These ideas are in keeping with those of the *Bullock Report*. By the age of 9 children should be able to 'use a specialised vocabulary for historical artefacts and events', 'use terms which permit ordering of events'; and 'describe events orally'.[21] Other approaches should be occasionally used but should not form the regular methods of teachers, since they involve extra effort and time. They include the use of artefacts, role-playing, model-making, and the use of radio and television.

The Use of Artefacts

Old objects, or good reproductions of them, are the true evidence of Time and Place for young children. They are particularly useful for the study of Time, for which genuine resources are less plentiful than Place. They also satisfy young children's collecting instinct. Certain artefacts, such as stamps, can be collected and kept by children to teach them about distant lands. Others have to be borrowed from museums if they are valuable or very old, or brought by teachers and children if they date from, say, late Victorian times. Energetic teachers can assemble a worthwhile school museum if a museum case with a lock can be found; this can be useful to many classes over the years.

Artefacts may be used throughout the 5 to 9 age-range equally effectively. Infants can sort old objects as to likely age and make a sequence-line showing which comes before which in time. Questions and discussions about one artefact make a stimulating introduction to any lesson. 7 to 9 children can use artefacts for display purposes on a table, and have coloured tapes from them to information they have discovered in written work on the display board. They are also a good way for children to find out how things work if the object is mechanised or can be used. Ancient toys are always a source of great joy to children of this age.[22] Detailed help with how to use artefacts is given by John Lally in relation to John West's work in Dudley schools.[23]

Role-playing

When children have enough information to discuss a particular topic, a good way to learn that information and make it part of themselves is to imagine an appropriate social problem or situation, take the parts of different people involved and discuss their respective points of view. This is a sure way to develop empathy and perhaps improve children's future ability to understand people. Role-play can also be used to revise a story told by the teacher, as in the formal situation of a role-play exercise. The first is more suitable for infants and the second for 7 to 9 age children. It has been suggested that children can imagine that they are running a farm over several years and have to decide which crops should be grown in which fields during which months of the year to give enough variety of produce to yield a profit.[24] This involves learning about farming and the whole class entering into the plans by discussion, with teacher leadership. A more definite and therefore easier role-play exercise is given in the ILEA pamphlet; the exercise is called 'Living in the Alps'.[25] In this, eight people of varying ages are faced with the threat of a big holiday camp being built in their quiet village; they discuss their reactions with the help of a diagrammatic map. This could be done with the class divided into groups of eight. A role-play concerned with time past might be for children to imagine that they live in a seventeenth-century town, look at a contemporary map of the few streets and discuss their everyday lives from the point of view of town officials such as scavengers, levelookers, the hayward and the sexton. One section of Liverpool Teaching Unit No. 3, giving extracts from the Liverpool Town Books, provides information for the port of Liverpool.[26] The problem of these people might be the Civil War and the arrival of Prince Rupert's troops in their port. The essentials of successful role-playing are detailed knowledge from the teacher and children's reading, simple resource material to help decisions, and efficient organisation of the class, with a final class discussion about decisions made by the groups. From my experience, simulation and gaming of a more sophisticated kind are not suitable for 5 to 9-year-old children.

Model-making

The concrete nature of models makes them an effective approach for all children of this age-range; they range from match-box buildings and toilet roll towers to more ambitious lay-outs of a village, town or monastery. For this active approach to learning to be effective, children should first learn about the particular model from pictures, slides and, if possible, reading. From the point of view of Time, the Quennell series of books are clearly illustrated with bold black and white sketches and provide detailed information about smaller items.[27] A beginning can be made with one or two children making one item for a bigger display, such as a ship for the model of a port. Eric Barker gives an illustration of the stages of making a cargo ship by 8 to 9-year-olds in the 1968 edition of his well-known book.[28] A village can also be modelled with each child providing a building. From this a beginning can be made to map work, especially if the model is part of the local scene and can be studied before field work is attempted. Detailed practical help with model-making is given for 5 to 9 age children by David Rowbotham. He distinguishes between landscape models, building/townscape models and working models.[29] The closest link between Time and models has been forged by E.E. Newton in his work at St Peter's School, Everton. This small school (JMI) in the heart of Liverpool based its topic work on Liverpool's history as portrayed in models.[30] Teachers should be wary of using this method for all their Place and Time work and a framework for the school should favour this method as an activity only at certain stages. They should also be careful to discuss with their class the relevance of the particular model and how it fits into the study of Place and Time for the year. The necessary attention to detail and practical efficiency in model-making could lead to inability to relate the model to a wider scene.

The Use of Radio and Television

As with the use of artefacts, role-playing and model-making, radio and television should be used sparingly, otherwise the method of teaching becomes the main concern rather than the learning of Place and Time. Schools vary tremendously in the technical support given to staff for listening and viewing. LEAs could provide libraries of tape-recordings of appropriate broadcasts which could be borrowed easily or even brought round the schools in the same way in which publishers' representatives circulate. In such ways teachers are encouraged to use broadcasts. In the same way, the practical side of having a television in your classroom when required or a video-recorder in your school alters the situation completely.[31] Schools blessed with these facilities will be able to use broadcasts and television programmes happily, though they may be tempted to use an excellent programme too consistently and even to repeat viewing it in different classes, if there is no framework for Place and Time.

Another caveat about broadcasts and television programmes is that they have been developed in the post Plowden era of 'one-off' topics and most of them cater for the unrelated topic approach. Therefore schools adopting a framework throughout the 5 to 9 years must be selective in using these programmes. They can promote inactivity and uncritical viewing unless teachers prepare well from the pamphlets provided and follow up the programme as suggested. These programmes are, however, excellent in every way and a tremendous support to the hard pressed non-specialist teacher. As in the case of field work, pre-paration, careful listening and viewing supported by simple workcards, and thorough follow-up and relationship to a scheme of work are neces-sary. Specific programmes will be discussed in Chapter 4.

These ten approaches to Place and Time, six basic ones and four effective 'extras' if the school situation allows their implementation, are normal methods of approach alongside the more specialised ones out-lined in the next two sections of this chapter. For example, mapping is closely connected with field work and specific geographical vocabu-lary with story-telling. Also, time charts are closely linked to recording of work by children, and historical fiction to story-telling.

Approaches More Specific to Place

These are weather study, graphicacy, and distant lands. They are not put in any particular order, since most of them are used constantly throughout work on Place and are of a developmental nature through-out the primary school.

Weather Study

Study of the weather is a continuous process in the 5 to 9 age-group, as later, but it takes a more specific form in the infant school. Very young children should be taught to observe the state of the weather and its changes each day, and also to record it simply as a classroom task for a rota of children. If 5-year-olds are shown a chart of some of the more obvious pictures meaning different types of weather, they can apply it very simply on a week's weather chart as in Figure 3.1. By the first year of the junior school (7 to 8) children should be able to work on a more complicated chart covering a month, as in Figure 3.2. In a useful chapter on 'Weather Studies' in the Geographical Association's handbook, Tim Firth suggests that 5 to 7-year-old children can learn about weather conditions by discussion of a 'Spring theme' as a topic,

Figure 3.1: Weather Chart for a Week (5-7s)

	Mon.	Tues.	Wed.	Thurs.	Fri.
Morning	 Rain				
Afternoon	 Showers				

Source: E.J. Barker, *The Junior Geography Lesson* (OUP, 1968), p. 82.

and also in discussion of snow and ice, rain, shade, wind, shelter and sun. He uses simple practical methods such as standing in the sun and dressing up warmly for frost as ways of teaching children. Development is evident in this work and he suggests that 8 to 9-year-olds could learn to read a thermometer and relate it to weather conditions. They can also learn about shadow, compass points (also related to map work), wind and cloud. Concentration on weather study in the 5 to 9 age range will enable its natural use in the later junior years, in reading and reference.

Graphicacy (Map Work)

Graphicacy is a modern blanket term for the ability to use graphs, diagrams, models, photographs and maps (which includes globes, atlases and other maps such as OS maps). The need for this skill is so great that it is now considered never too young to start learning. In the words of G.H. Gopsill, 'Children should be brought up to regard a map as a document which describes a living landscape'.[32] So much has been written recently about how to teach the skill of graphicacy that the space at my disposal prevents detailed reference, and I therefore suggest that teachers read one or more of the following books and articles:

D Boardman. *Graphicacy and Geography Teaching* (Croom Helm, 1983)

S.J. Catling. 'Maps and Cognitive Maps: The Young Child's Perception,' *Geography* (November 1979)

M. Harris. *Starting from Maps, Schools Council Environmental Studies Project 5-13*, Teacher's Guide and Case Studies (Hart-Davis, 1972)

Figure 3.2: Weather Chart for a Month (7 to 9s)

JULY 1983

Sun.	31	3	10	17	24
Mon.		4	11	18	25
Tues.		5	12	19	26
Wed.		6	13	20	27
Thurs.		7	14	21	28
Fri.	1	8	15	22	29
Sat.	2	9	16	23	30

Snow	Hail	Rain	Storm	Rainbow	Fog	Wind	Cloud	Sun

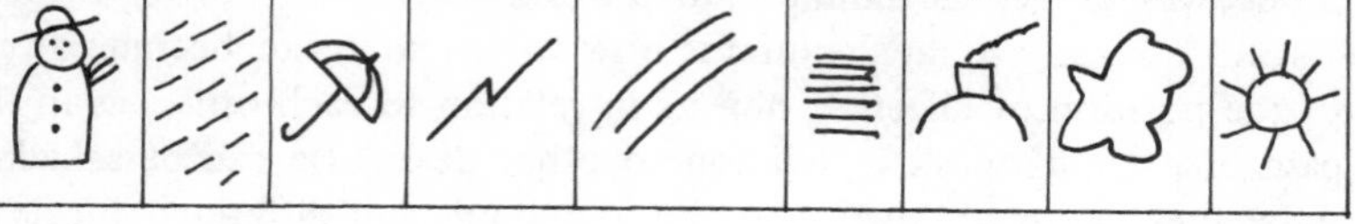

Sources: G.H. Gopsill, *The Teaching of Geography* (Macmillan, 1958), p. 31; D. Mills (ed.), *Geographical Work in Primary and Middle Schools* (Geographical Association, 1981), p. 21.

ILEA *The Study of Places in the Primary School* (1981) (OS maps and aerial photographs pp. 32-3)

D. Mills, (ed.) *Geographical Work in Primary and Middle Schools* (Geographical Association, 1981) (Maps and Mapping, pp. 98-122)

P. Prosser, *The World on Your Doorstep* (McGraw-Hill, 1982) pp. 121-7

M. Cribb, *Introducing Maps 5-13* (National Association of Environmental Education, 1982)

In all these publications the objectives have been to get children to observe accurately (interpreting their observations), to read maps correctly (making comparisons between them), to record information, and finally to draw their own maps. These are difficult, if very useful, skills only to be acquired gradually over many years. Graphicacy skills hoped for by the age of 7 and the age of 9 are given in Figure 3.3.[33]

Infants have less dexterity than lower juniors and this must be considered when embarking on these skills, so as not to daunt them too easily. They are naturally untidy in drawing pictures and recording information, but this does not matter as long as the skill is being developed. Success should be gauged by understanding rather than neatness. The ruler has often to be abandoned for the piece of string or side of a piece of paper, for measuring. One of the first geographers to believe that infants liked maps was Michael Storm, now Staff Inspector in Geography for ILEA. Since his interest in this type of work with infants, other workers have found that young children understand their environment from pictures and aerial photographs. Perfect teaching technique is to be found in *Playing with Plans* by Michael Storm.[34] This is a short book to be read by infants. It has large pictures and plans on each page with short sentences telling a story about a family having a house built; all the problems they meet are eventually solved by plans. It clearly explains the words 'scale drawing' and 'centimetres'. Susan Lynn and Caroline Wilson experimented with infants in a Croydon school and found that starting with a picture map and moving onto a model was the best beginning to map work.[35]

Still others have taught infants how to 'orientate' or become aware of the position of different objects in relation to each other, as in the case of a child's desk in relation to other desks. He can be asked to draw the top of his own desk, his notebook and different objects in relation to it as in Figure 3.4.[36] Children of 5 to 7 also have to become accustomed to how different objects look viewed sideways as well as from above. They usually need to have an outline given to them before they can complete a diagram; for example they can put chairs, tables, and other furniture into a classroom outline if the pieces of furniture are named for inclusion. A development of this is to map the points of

Figure 3.3: Graphicacy Skills

Age 5-7

By the age of 7 children should normally be able to:

1. Follow directions using left, right, forwards, in a circle, etc.
2. Describe the relative locations of objects using before, behind, in front of, to the left of, etc.
3. Sort objects by relative size and draw round them.
4. Sort objects by their shapes, such as squares, circles, etc. and draw round them.
5. Draw round life-size objects such as coins, pencils, toys, etc. to show their shapes in plan form.
6. Draw routes between objects drawn, such as the path of an imaginary crawling insect.
7. Draw symbols to illustrate picture maps or imaginary maps.
8. Measure spaces between objects using hands or feet.

Age 7-9

By the age of 9 children should normally be able to:

9. Plot the cardinal directions NESW.
10. Use a compass to find NESW in the school playground.
11. Draw a plan at a very large scale, such as a desk top with objects on it.
12. Measure from a large scale plan, such as a teacher-prepared plan of the classroom.
13. Insert in their approximate positions on the plan objects in the room, such as blackboard, cupboards.
14. Record around the plan features seen from the room, such as playground, trees.
15. Draw free-hand a map showing a simple route, such as the journey to school.
16. Make a simple model of part of the neighbourhood such as a row of shops.
17. Give locations in grid squares, such as A1, B3, etc. as on an A to Z road map.
18. Measure straight line distances between two points on an A to Z road map.
19. Draw some conventional symbols on an imaginary map and add a key.
20. Identify different countries shown on atlas maps.

Source: D. Boardman, *Graphicacy and Geography Teaching* (Croom Helm, 1983), p. 168.

Figure 3.4: My Desk (5-7 years)   Figure 3.5: Sign post map (5-7 years)

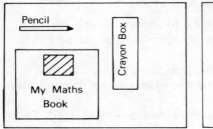
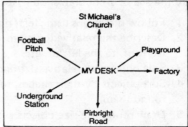

Source: D. Mills (ed.), *Geographical Work in Primary and Middle Schools* (Geographical Association, 1981), pp. 103-4.

the compass (North, South, East, West), starting from each child using his own hands for direction, and then using a piece of paper. Left/right directions can also be learnt in this way, together with themselves in relation to their environment (Figure 3.5).[37]

When work has been regularly undertaken on orientation through plans in the 5 to 7 age-range, young juniors can begin work on routes, perhaps when studying the topic of 'Transport'. Roger Cracknell gives an interesting exercise on how the coalman delivers coal to various homes. The children are asked to work out the shortest route for the coalman to each home using a piece of string measuring 100 metres (Figure 3.6).[38] Eric Barker in a similar way makes up a workcard using an imaginary map of a locality round a school; children of 8 to 9 are given six tasks to undertake in relation to the map (Figure 3.7).[39] During the fourth year of our age-range children should be introduced to the OS map by using 50″ to the mile maps and later 25″ to the mile maps, at first covering a small local area. The ILEA pamphlet reminds us that the larger the scale of map the smaller the area covered and therefore the more detail is shown. A good way to teach OS use is to read *The Map That Came to Life*[40] as a picture story about Joanne and John (and Rover the dog) walking to the fair with the help of a 1″ to the mile OS map specially enlarged for the book.

Throughout the 5 to 9 age-range aerial photographs of increasing

Figure 3.6: Coalyard and Coal Buyers' Homes

x buyers' homes

0   100
metres

Note: The plan shows the coalyard, and several streets in a town. Mr Snow, the coalman, has to deliver coal to each of the houses marked with a X.

(a) Draw what you think is the best route for him and his lorry to take. (Tracing paper could be placed over the plan or the teacher could duplicate copies of the plan)

(b) Place a piece of string against the scale shown. Put one end on the 'O' and where the string passes the line marking the '100' make a mark. Cut the string at this point. This represents 100 metres on the ground. Using this length of string, measure how long the route is that you have chosen for Mr Snow. Find out from all those in the class who has the shortest route.

Source: J.R. Cracknell, *Teaching Geography through Topics in Primary and Middle Schools* (Geographical Association, 1979), p. 22.

Figure 3.7: Workcard for Introducing Children to Printed Maps

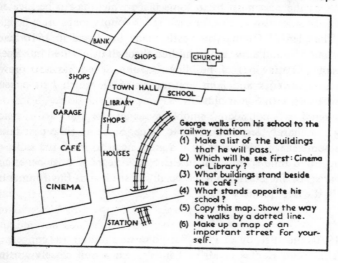

Source: E.J. Barker, *The Junior Geography Lesson* (OUP, 1968), p. 71.

complexity may be used for teaching change in the landscape. Vertical photographs show the building or landscape as a plan. For example, a study of Edward I's Welsh castles is best started from looking at Rhuddlan Castle, Harlech Castle and Beaumaris Castle from the air; this clearly shows the increasing sophistication of Edward's building.[41] Oblique photographs show a different view taken when the aeroplane is lower down; comparison of vertical and oblique is very instructive. Comparison of plans and maps is of course one of the skills we are seeking in map work. The ILEA pamphlet is helpful about this type of teaching aid (p. 33).

As each primary school child should have his own dictionary (suitably graded) for general use, so he should also have access to a globe in his earlier years, and a simple atlas from about the age of 7. An atlas is one of the tools of the trade for Place as the sequence/time-line is for Time. By the age of 7 a child should be able to use an atlas if the previous years have been spent as suggested, getting used to orientation, diagrams, plans and routes. Constant early reference to globe and atlas by the teacher, and in the tasks set for children, accustoms pupils to learn how to use the index, and in later junior years reference grids for 'co-ordinates' (i.e., the point where two reference lines meet on the map) for finding exact places. The study of Time benefits from all this work as the past must be in some place which has to be located. John Speed's inset town maps for each of his county maps are a delight to use. The plan of Caernarvon Castle made by Speed in 1610 leads to many queries, and appeals to children through its labelled buildings, street plan and drawings of buildings.[42] John Speed has also drawn similar plans of York and Southampton in 1610, which I have used most effectively with 6-year-olds.[43]

Although I have considered graphicacy as an essential part of Place teaching it is hardly less important to Time. Since all time past takes place in some place, historians have a great need to learn the skills of graphicacy, and time spent on it in the 5 to 9 years is most beneficial in both areas of the curriculum, especially if studied as Environmental Studies in the later primary years.

Distant Lands

In the 1930s much study of Place for younger children was concerned with 'People and Homes in Many Lands' from a dull closely-written textbook illustrated by a minimum of black and white photographs. Since then, particularly in the last fifteen years, the tide has turned to give great emphasis to environmental and local study. The need for international understanding, and the movement among geographers to make all study of Place global has initiated schemes which include distant lands at some stage (see schemes of work in Chapter 2). This is made easier in multi-cultural schools where the children themselves are the living artefacts of distant lands. From his research John Carnie considers that up to the age of 11 the majority of children are tolerant of each other and see people from other countries as more like themselves than unlike them. He recommends the purposeful use of stories from other countries in the 5 to 9 age-range;[44] (reference has already been made to the bibliography of story books on pp. 34-5 of the ILEA pamphlet). Television programmes concerned with other places should also be used when appropriate.[45] Television has made all children more immediately aware of their importance, and in some cases this has been reinforced by holidays abroad.

An example of work with 4 to 5-year-olds on India involves the concrete approach of discussing Indian artefacts such as saris, pipes, paper snakes, jewellery, pictures of Mother Theresa and a talk from a Hindu teacher.[46] Another teacher undertook a project on Botswana with 6-year-olds. This involved a visit to the Commonwealth Institute, slides and a film from Oxfam, the sorting of pictures of Botswana animals and other practical work, all displayed for parents. A class of 8 to 9-year-olds at a London junior school made a film called 'Sharing' in which the children were shown sharing in the classroom, school and eventually in the Third World.[47] All these would need considerable preparation on the part of the teacher and it is to be hoped that these resources could be used in future years, particulary the film of 'Sharing'. More detailed topic-type work is suggested by Roger Cracknell,[48] and this involves family life, climate, agriculture and the city. It is intended for all primary age children and suggests different work for younger and older juniors. It starts with children's own families and comparison of them with an Indian family, and continues with activities on agriculture, climate and the city of Bombay. This work involves the preparation of several plans and maps as well as other resources, including the accumulation of books. It should form an integral part of any 7 to 9 age scheme, to be repeated each year.

Although preparation of work for the 5 to 9-year-olds on distant countries is at first time-consuming, more help will be given with resources in the next chapter. Teachers should include some aspect of this work in their schemes and gradually build up resources, avoiding India being studied both in the reception class and with 8 to 9-year-olds. As there is so much interest taken in multi-cultural education by those in authority 'holding the purse strings', as well as general interest in world politics, more resources should be forthcoming. This may in fact be a better resourced area than many others in the Place/Time curriculum.

Approaches More Specific to Time

These are sequence-lines, time-charts and time clocks;[49] family trees; oral history; and historical fiction. All have links with Place. The skill of understanding and making time-charts and family trees is linked to graphicacy, because it involves the ability to comprehend events, names and dates in relationship to each other in diagrammatic space. Oral history is usually thought of as a source of finding out about how people lived in the recent past (the last eighty years) but interviews with old people from different countries can be useful for work in Place. Historical fiction also has its links with Place since many stories suitable for young children involve diagrams and maps. Examples of this come in A.A. Milne's *Winnie the Pooh*, Michael Bond's *Paddington Bear*, R.L. Stevenson's *Treasure Island* and Daniel Defoe's *Robinson Crusoe*.

Sequence-lines, Time-charts and Time Clocks

Until the late 1970s many research workers and teachers believed that Time was impossible for children of 5 to 9 to understand, so that 'the past' was a closed book to them. Even as late as 1979 Michael Storm, sympathetic towards the study of the past with young children, spoke of 'the young child's fragile chronological sense'.[50] Research done since then, notably by John West, has altered this point of view and teachers are now being encouraged to *teach* time by using graded sequence-lines and charts as well as time clocks from the age of 6. As in many other skills this teaching should be a continuing activity introduced into all work in class, and constant reference should be made to class and individual lines/charts.

In the years 5 to 7 a start should be made on sequence-lines in a study of the Family. If the teacher is bold enough to give her own 'life-line' on a visual aid or blackboard she can show how small the 5/6 years of the children's lines are compared with her own life. I favour horizontal lines up to the age of 9 as they are not so easily confused with North and South of the compass points in a vertical line. Children of this age are also learning to write from the left-hand side of the page

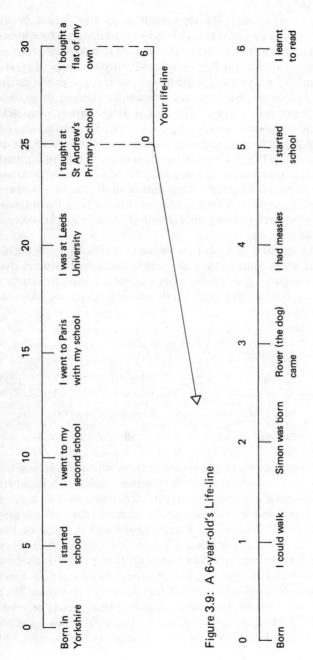

Figure 3.8: An Adult Life-line

Figure 3.9: A 6-year-old's Life-line

to the right-hand side. Therefore such a 'life-line' might be as in Figure 3.8. Discussion of this could lead to the children's own lives and they could each make their own, with the help of a duplicated one with notches made by the teacher. Number is involved here. Figure 3.9 is an example of a 6-year-old's 'life-line'. If writing proves too difficult, the numbered sequence-line on its own allows children to talk about what has happened to them. The real difficulty arises with lack of memory and it is often advisable to involve willing parents, who come into school and help their children. The main importance of this type of work is to teach an understanding of sequence (not dates), that is, what event comes before or after another. The children's life-lines should be fastened into their Time Books or Books of the Past for later reference. As John West emphasises, the aim is to teach the commonsense of 'order', since an understanding of historical time depends upon correct sequence.

From the age of 7 onwards time-lines and eventually time-charts can be used with every topic of the past studied. Short depth studies are the easiest as a beginning, since the length of time involved is small. For example the line in Figure 3.10 shows fifty years of Elizabethan England:

Figure 3.10: Time-line of Elizabethan England

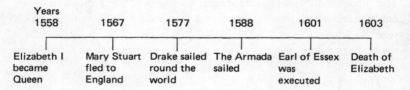

This is a sequence-line and the spaces between the dates do not represent years. Although many of the themes studied in Elizabethan England are social ones which happen right through the reign, the important names and dates shown can be related to them. For example, a study of the Court involves Francis Drake and the Earl of Essex, though not Mary Stuart, who was a prisoner and did not have a court of her own (even though she was a Queen). Hence the introduction of specialised vocabulary is needed; 'the Court' in Elizabethan times is an élite circle of the Queen and her friends as well as a name for law courts where judges sit. These short sequence lines should be kept on the middle double-page spread of each child's notebook as well as being shown on a larger, perhaps more detailed, line at the back of the classroom. Onto this, children can fasten their own pictures, cut-outs and written work in the correct area. The notebooks should be taken on to the 8 to 9 class for reference in relation to the next part of the past studied, though the class sequence line will remain in the old classroom.

In the second year of the junior school longer and more detailed time-lines should be made in the same way, but the class time-line should include, for example, the Elizabethan England line on a small scale in relation to the new year's topics, however distant in time they are to one another. Exact, correctly measured time-lines are not appropriate in the primary school. The second year time-line might look like Figure 3.11.

Figure 3.11: Time-line of Modern England

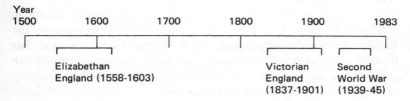

The brackets containing the topics studied should be coloured in different crayons or paints. The important factor here is the knowledge that teachers have of work done in the other classes, and the reference made, through time-lines, to work done earlier in school. This gives structure and relevance to Time study.

Throughout the 5 to 9 age-range time clocks are another space dimension to the teaching of Time. While children are learning to tell the time and using a large clock face with movable hands, it is possible to teach one of the smallest parts of 'time past' by using a time clock to illustrate the day in the life of a medieval peasant or monk, a British slave building Hadrian's Wall or a modern MP. This exercise could start with the child's day in school on a clock face and then develop into a person in another age and the difference in their lives. For example, the peasant rose at day-break and went to bed when the sun went down, whereas the MP often works into the early hours of the morning. Children are learning to tell the time as well as learning about the past.

John West's research on time will influence scheme construction in a number of important ways. For example, he found that 7 to 9-year-old children could correctly sequence pictures of long distant objects and events (such as a fossil, the pyramids and the crucifixion) more easily than very recent ones. They also found it difficult to sequence events backwards beyond the lives of their grandparents. This may suggest the contention that younger children understand early civilizations better than more recent times and that a regressive approach to teaching juniors is not very effective.[51] But he does not therefore advocate a purely chronological syllabus of 'Early Man' for 7-year-olds, and so on. In fact he favours the non-chronological approach as it makes both teacher and children use time-charts to see where their particular topic comes into the past. He also links the understanding of time to historical language development, since children cannot understand the time without using words such as 'decade', 'century', 'period', 'old', 'recent' and so on. John Lally provides us with an excellent summary of John West's research on time in his *Teachers' Guide*.[52]

Family Trees

Family relationships in the present and the past loom large in all our lives. 'Blood is stronger than water' dies hard and this fact of life is a great motivator of events in the past, particularly when studying royalty. Family trees are a conventional form of making these relationships concise and clear and they can take several forms. Young children of 5 to 7 sometimes find it easier to start from the right-hand side of the page as the time nearest to them and work to the left, in boxes, to their grandparents. Figure 3.12 shows an imaginative example of one of this type:

Figure 3.12: My Family Plan (5-7 years)

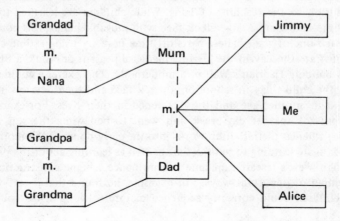

This is a beginning, using the child's own family, but it can be developed in later infant years by turning the page, so to speak, so that your grandparents come at the top, which is how an historical family tree is made and used, without the boxes, using lines only. The present Royal Family could form the next link and eventually one could get back in the 7 to 9 age-range to the Tudor dynasty depicted as in Figure 3.13:

Figure 3.13: Tudor Royal Family Tree

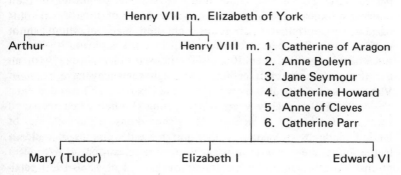

Again here are three 'generations' (new word), depicted as in our own families, with the additional technique of adding Roman numerals to the kings and queens. This involves the time factor as well, since Henry VII is 'older' than the others and living a 'longer time back'. Family-trees teach time and in this case relationships and Henry VIII's dynastic problems. (Why did Henry have so many wives?) The teacher will have to draw the guiding lines and put the names on the blackboard for insertion in the correct places.

More will be said about resources for this type of work in the next chapter but a simple example of a pictorial family tree showing the Fisher family and the Cooper family is given in *Two Victorian Families* in the *People Around Us Series*.[53] These books are suitable for 6 to 9-year-olds. Two to three generations of the Stonor family, living in the fifteenth century at Stonor Park, Oxfordshire, are given in simple family trees in *The Stonors*, a family history patch study.[54] This book and others in the same series are suitable for 8 to 9-year-olds to read for themselves and for teachers to read in story time to younger children. They are full of contemporary illustrations and good photographs.

A family tree is a quick form of showing relationships in a limited space and this Time technique is no more difficult than a diagram or large teacher-made map in Place study. It should be developed at an early age as a normal form of giving and recording information, and teachers of young children should not fear it as a teaching medium.

Oral History

Oral history is historical evidence gained through talking to older people about their knowledge of the past. During the 1960s it became a respectable branch of academic history in the universities and has now passed to teachers in the schools. Its very nature as the means of transmission of knowledge about the past by word of mouth, makes it particularly appropriate with younger children, many of whom cannot read or write. The period of the past it involves is obviously limited, since people aged between 70 and 80 and even older can only remember the past during this century, although they may have heard of Victorian and Edwardian days through their parents and grandparents. Yet it is the last eighty years which young children can understand from the Time point of view. Teachers should ensure that schemes of work include these years and that suitable older friends of children in the school are regularly introduced into the classroom as live pieces of historical evidence. I have found the period of 1880-1980 particularly easy to teach to top infants; not only is it a 'century' but other resources besides older friends are plentiful and colourful.[55]

The detailed method of approach should be carefully worked out and the same procedure be adopted by all teachers in the same school. Care should be taken to invite people suitable for your particular topic, otherwise discussion can become too far-flung. For example, in the period 1900 to 1980, topics might be 'Edwardian Schooldays 1901-10', 'Women's Work in the Home 1918-38' or 'The Second World War 1939-45' ('On the Home Front' or 'In the Forces'). The children should have been taught about the topic before the older people come to school, particular questions should be prepared and written down for specific children to ask, and the older people prepared for the slant of the interview, so that they can collect old photographs, letters and artefacts to illustrate their replies. If the old people have small voices several people should be invited at once, and the class divided into groups. In this way the visitors can move round the groups. If these friends are willing to talk into a tape-recorder their knowledge can be gone over later and much more work done on it. In any case the interviews (better than an 'open-ended talk' from a visitor) should be used by the teacher afterwards, by incorporating them into the topic in hand, with the children recording the event in some way in their notebooks. All teachers in the school should know which old people are being asked so that certain ones are not used too much. This method of approach may be used throughout the 5 to 9 age-range though the older children can do more work themselves and take the initiative in asking questions.

Oral history is a method frequently used for the study of family history. The most relevant experiment for our age-range is that done by Sallie Purkis with a class of 7 to 8-year-olds. She involved the children's grandmothers in answering a short questionnaire and lending artefacts in a bigger topic of 'Milton Road Junior School in Edwardian Days'. In this case the grandmothers talked to their own grandchildren in the class and came to the school for an afternoon with the children's parents. A real family affair![56] More examples of work done with infants and older children may be found in other books.[57]

Historical Fiction

During the last twenty years a prolific number of historical novels have been published and many of them are suitable for 5 to 9-year-old children if they are read to them selectively by the teacher, or the story summarised, with certain passages read.[58] This is a good store of detailed historical information which can be read in story-time to 7 to 9-year-old children. As they require some knowledge of the period of the past depicted, the teacher is well-advised to select novels with whose period she is familiar. In many of these the author is so knowledgeable about the period that she yields more authentic detail than other History books.[59]

Another use for historical novels is for the teacher to select a short passage of highly imaginative writing which the children read with her from a duplicated sheet, before trying to continue the story in their own words. It is interesting for children to know the actual story continued by the author, so this should be read by the teacher to them later. This is only suitable for 8 to 9-year-olds, and not all of these. Some of this age-group can read some of the shorter stories for themselves and tell the rest of the class about them. Suitable stories are often about children's adventures such as Alison Utley's *Travellers in Time* (Puffin) and Geoffrey Trease's *The Children Crusade* (Longman, Penguin and the Bodley Head). Vivid and active passages of books usually give such detail that after a reading and re-reading, role-playing of the scene can be done, with children even using the actual words of the novel if they each have a duplicated passage. Artistic work can also be done of lively and memorable scenes from a selected descriptive passage. Some publishers have illustrated the novels boldly and attractively, so that even non-readers can understand the story from the illustrations.

The object of historical fiction is to portray the excitement of an historical story by depicting the feelings and activities of the people involved. But they are also related to Place as the descriptions of the settings of these novels is true and detailed. As Carolyn Horovitz says 'the historical novel differs from all other forms of novel in its characteristic use of time and place'.[60] Therefore a novel about the English Civil War must be placed in some particular part of England, which is described in detail. In this way historical fiction is a natural integrating factor for teachers of Place and Time and should not be neglected.

Although I have discussed ten approaches common to Place and Time, three additional ones for Place and four for Time, very few teachers will be able to use them all, even during the four years of the 5 to 9 age-range. Restrictions are placed on teachers by class size, the school's environment, lack of resources, the authority of the head teacher and lack of time to prepare adequately. In this age-range teachers may also be restricted by a colleague in charge of Social Studies/Humanities who is authoritarian enough to insist on certain methods. If a teacher herself is in charge of this area of the curriculum she may find other colleagues unwilling to use a variety of methods. Most of these approaches can be used with any scheme of work, though obviously a local study must involve field work. Some approaches are more suitable for infants than 8 to 9-year-olds but teachers of all age-groups are advised to try out seemingly more difficult methods with younger children, since recent research has found that most primary school children need to be 'stretched' intellectually more than they are at present.[61] In family (vertically) grouped classes, or classes of mixed ages (owing to a decrease in school numbers), several methods might have to be used with different groups of children. For example, while one group is recording a story in pictures and writing, another group might be role-playing that story in another part of the room. Although teachers are encouraged to use as great a variety of method as possible, some may find a few well-tried methods suit their class very well. Yet a responsible person should try to ensure that a variety of methods is used during the four years under consideration. When a scheme of work is finally evolved for a school, suggestions as to the best approaches for each age-range should be written in brackets near the topic.

Notes

1. J. Tough, *Talking and Learning* (Ward Lock, 1977).
2. R. Clayfield, 'Back to first principles', *Times Educational Supplement* (11 June 1982).
3. J. Lally and J. West, *The Child's Awareness of the Past*, Teachers' Guide (Hereford and Worcester County History Advisory Committee, 1981), pp. 6-7.
4. J.E. Blyth, *History in Primary Schools* (McGraw-Hill, 1982), pp. 65-72.
5. *The Study of Places in the Primary School* (ILEA Guidelines, 1981), pp. 34-5.
6. P.J. Rogers, *The New History* (Historical Association, T.H. 44, 1979), p. 8.
7. R. Unwin, *The Visual Dimension in the Study and Teaching of History* (Historical Association, T.H. 49, 1981), p. 5.
8. G. Elliott, *The Oxford New Geography, a course for juniors*, Book 2 (OUP, 1980), p. 80-1.
9. See B. Clark (ed.), *The Changing World in the Primary School* (ILEA, 1981), p. 26 for an example.
10. See Lally and West.
11. R. Lavender, 'Children Using Information Books', *Education 5-13*, vol. 11, no. 1 (Spring 1983).
12. An account of 'Kingswood' by M. West may be found in J.E. Blyth, *History in Primary Schools* (McGraw-Hill, 1982), p. 101-2.
13. D. Rowbotham, 'Can We Do Field Work in Primary Schools?' *Teaching Geography*, vol. 8, no. 2 (October 1982).
14. See Chapter 6 for an account of the visit.
15. S. Scoffham, *Using the School's Surroundings: A Guide to Local Studies in Urban Schools* (Ward Lock, 1980).
16. H. Pluckrose, *Let's Use the Locality* (Mills and Boon, 1971).
17. D. Milburn, 'Children's Vocabulary', in N. Graves (ed.) *New Movements in the Study and Teaching of Geography* (Temple Smith, 1972).
18. *New Thinking in Geography* (HMSO, 1972).
19. Melanie Harvey, 'Geography with 5 to 7-year-olds', in D. Mills (ed.) *Geographical Work in Primary and Middle Schools* (Geographical Association, 1981).
20. J.B. Colthan, 'Junior School children's understanding of some terms commonly used in the teaching of History', unpublished PhD thesis, Manchester University, 1960.
21. Lally and West.
22. The Museum of London, Bethnall Green, London, houses an excellent collection.
23. Lally and West, pp. 8-10.
24. *New Thinking in Geography*, p. 14.
25. *The Study of Places in the Primary School*.
26. *A Town under Siege: Liverpool in the Civil War 1642-4* (Liverpool Teaching Unit no. 3, 1978).
27. M. and CHB. Quennell, *History of Everyday Things in England* (Batsford, 1954-68).
28. E.J. Barker, *The Junior Geography Lesson* (OUP, 1968), Figure 2, p. 15.
29. D. Rowbotham, 'Hardware models' in Mills (ed.).
30. E.E. Newton, 'An Evertonian Spilling Over', *Teaching History*, vol. 1, no. 4 (1970).
31. All ILEA schools have their own video recorders. Many also have computers, which are most useful with older children.
32. G.H. Gopsill, *The Teaching of Geography* (Macmillan, 1958), p. 59.

33. Taken from D. Boardman, *Graphicacy and Geography Teaching* (Croom Helm, 1983), p. 168.

34. M. Storm, *Playing with Plans* (Longman, 1974).

35. S. Lynn and C. Wilson, 'Discovering Maps', *Child Education*, (May, 1980).

36. Taken from Mills (ed.), Figures 5, 6, p. 104.

37. Ibid. Figure 5.2, p. 103.

38. Taken from J.R. Cracknell, *Teaching Geography through Topics in Primary and Middle Schools* (Geographical Association, 1979), Figure 2.7, p. 22.

39. Taken from E.J. Barker, *The Junior Geography Lesson* (OUP, 1968), Figure 17, p. 71.

40. H.J. Deverson, *The Map That Came to Life* (OUP, 1967).

41. P.H. Humphries, *Castles of Edward the First in Wales* (HMSO, 1983). Aerial photographs of Rhuddlan (p. 33), Harlech (p. 47) and Beaumaris (p. 59) may be obtained from the castle sites as postcards or slides.

42. Ibid., p. 18.

43. See Blyth, Figures 3, 4, pp. 76-7.

44. J. Carnie, 'The growth of junior children's ideas of nations and races', *General Studies Association Bulletin* no. 13 (Summer 1969).

45. M.J. Storm, 'Children's Images of Other Countries: the Influence of the Media' in Clark (ed.).

46. Adults from distant lands, if carefully selected, are often willing to come into school and answer prepared questions.

47. Examples taken from Mills (ed.), pp. 128-9.

48. See Cracknell, pp. 39-56.

49. For fuller treatment see Blyth, pp. 112-23.

50 Storm, p. 12.

51. M. Pollard advocates teaching history backwards in his *History for Juniors* (Evans, 1973).

52. Lally and West, p. 30-3.

53. S. Wagstaff, *Two Victorian Families*, (A and C Black, 1978).

54. P.J. Jefferies, *The Stonors* (Nelson, 1978) (See also *The Steels*, *The Lloyds* and *The Logans*).

55. See Chapter 6, Unit I, Croxteth Hall.

56. S. Purkis, 'An Experiment in Family History with First Year Juniors', *Teaching History*, vol. IV, no. 15 (May 1976).

57. Blyth, pp. 174-84; D.J. Steel and L. Taylor, *Family History in Schools* (Phillimore, 1973).

58. G. McBride (ed.), *A Catalogue of Children's Historical Novels* (Teachers' Centre, Queen's University, Belfast, 1976).

59. Recent examples of this are C. Harnett, *The Woolpack* (Methuen) and *Ring out Bow Bells* (Pelican), as recommended by S. Gregory, 'Recent Children's Historical Fiction', *Developments in History Teaching* J. Nichol (ed.) (School of Education, University of Exeter, 1980).

60. C. Horovitz, 'Dimensions in Time: a critical review of Historical fiction', *Horn Book Reflections* E.W. Field (ed.) (Boston 1969).

61. M. Donaldson, *Children's Minds*, Fontana, 1978.

4 RESOURCES FOR ACTIVITY

One reason why teachers have hesitated to use Place and Time in a structured way in the curriculum is the paucity of appropriate materials for their activity in these areas. The maxim that young children, and many older pupils and adults, learn best by 'doing' or experiencing, cannot be denied, but the study of places outside the school, often in distant countries, and the study of times and people both far away in time and place, presents difficulties in the very nature of the subject areas. Many educationalists in the past have therefore dismissed Place and Time as too difficult; no publishers or commercial firms have provided materials which children could use. This is a real problem and has led many good teachers to limit Place to a study of the near environment and not to tackle Time at all. Enthusiastic teachers have of course created their own resources, and to some extent this will always be the case, but more needs to be done commercially, and teachers of 5 to 9-year-olds need much support from specialists. When Place and Time gain a sure footing in the curriculum and teachers demand materials, publishers will react accordingly. There should always be a teacher responsible for Humanities work in First Schools with an allowance allotted to this work; she should collect and dispense resources as required in the school as a whole. Adapting materials suitable for children aged 9 to 13 is possible, especially if what is used is well-illustrated and used by bright 8 to 9-year-olds but adaptation is time-consuming and the whole process impractical with infant-age children.

When appropriate material has been collected, young children cannot be left to 'discover' at will, but need to have their work structured and organised by the teacher much more thoroughly than with older pupils. In the words of D.P. Ausubel and F.G. Robinson:[1]

Learning by discovery — in our opinion — does not necessarily lead to orderly, integrated and viable organisation, transformation and use of knowledge. It does so only in so far as the learning situation is highly structured, simplified and skilfully programmed . . . one must, in all fairness, attribute these latter outcomes to *the teachers' organisation of the data* from which the discovery is made, than to the act of discovery itself.

I italicise the reference to teachers since the materials to be discussed in this chapter must be selectively used and organised for particular age-ranges as for mixed age-groups, as appropriate. In my work on Croxteth Hall (see Chapter 6) I supplied much information and considerable material resources to the teacher of the class from which I withdrew my small group. Examples of this are the time-line of the Sefton family; visual aids of Croxteth Hall and fashion-mounted on coloured paper; slides from the Hall; a Victorian children's tea-set for display; a folder from Merseyside Museum called *The Rich and Poor in 19th Century Liverpool*[2] as well as a box of general books borrowed from various local libraries. From this, as I have written in Unit I, the skilled and experienced teacher of infants developed my narrower theme of Croxteth Hall to embrace poor as well as rich, and the topic of houses, present and past generally. This particular teacher said that this would have been impossible without my help and that the teacher of young children needs resources and advice about them more than anything else.

As the accessibility of all resources varies almost from year to year any advice has to be checked with publishers' catalogues, BBC radio and television programmes, museums and art galleries and commercial and charitable firms which provide materials free. A useful general book is *Treasure Chest for Teachers*, first published in 1960 and reprinted at least eleven times since then.[3]

Since Place and Time are information subjects needing many of the same skills and concepts for understanding and successful use, I will consider the common resources needed by both, including books, field work, illustrations, film, slides and film-strips, and then the more specialised resources needed for each. As a help to understanding the structure of the chapter I have made Figure 4.1, The Pyramid of Resources for Place and Time. At the top of the pyramid must be the teacher, the most valuable resource and also the most adaptable, as a human being. In order of priority, the resources Place and Time have in common are maps and time-lines, illustrative material, books (both for children and teachers), going out of school for field work and visits, and then the less essential but important three categories detailed, below the line, on the chart. Apparatus is a specialised resource for Place, and family and oral history for Time.

Figure 4.1: The Pyramid of Resources for Place and Time
(in comparative order of importance)

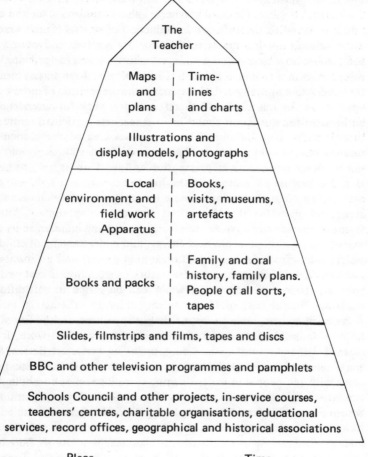

Note: ———— denotes division between basic and extra resources

The Teacher

The staffing problems of schools in 1983 have made this key resource a constant problem for head teachers. Falling numbers since the mid-1970s have led to the enforced introduction of vertical (family) grouping in schools not favourable to this type of organisation. Not only has the teacher now to contend with mixed-ability classes (some being very mixed even in a small class) but in addition, mixed-age classes in the 5 to 7 and 7 to 9 age-ranges. This has meant the preparation of more varied approaches for one class and therefore more work for teachers. The enthusiasm for this is not found in most teachers particularly now that promotion is more difficult. The Humanities area of the curriculum, unlike Number and Language, has suffered from lack of promotion, yet it entails more work in preparation and marking. It is to be hoped that the increase of numbers in the Infant School from 1985 onwards will necessitate more teachers and better organisation of schools so that some specialists for the Humanities area can be appointed. Without seeming to state the obvious, the teacher of young children must have knowledge, enthusiasm, physical energy, and understanding of children, adaptability, commonsense, good organising powers and a capacity for hard work. In addition to all these virtues (uncommon in one person), she must have a pleasant voice which can be varied to suit different occasions. In the case of Place she should have mathematical inclinations, such as being able to invent simple apparatus, and be fit enough to be responsible for a class of children on a day's field work. In the case of Time she must like reading, including historical fiction, have some sense of historical chronology and be able to develop good relations with old people in order to bring them into school. In both cases the artistic talent to draw and artistic sense to display children's work to advantage, must be included. It is no wonder that Place and Time have been neglected areas of the curriculum in view of the personal and professional demands made on the teacher. Let us hope that greater interest in younger children in relation to Place and Time and better staffing will improve- prospects for such teachers. Recent press criticisms of the teaching of Place and Time in HMI Reports may help to speed up this improvement.

Besides herself, the teacher should make more use of the blackboard and exposition of a topic on it. Two boards for each classroom are needed, as material may often be kept on one while the other is used for different sorts of work. Some schools, built ten to fifteen years ago, have no blackboards, which throws an additional burden onto teachers if they want to give an illustrated oral lesson or even write up difficult words for children. Magic-marker and white cartridge paper may be used but, in these times of economy, this is rather wasteful unless the work is to be kept for another time. There is still inadequate display space in most classrooms and this is essential for the constant use of sequence and time-lines to be kept up throughout the year, and for the regular display of maps.

An obvious but vital resource in schools is plenty of white and coloured paper and card of all shapes and sizes, for backing visual aids, making workbooks, acting as a base for the display of artefacts, and even for simple model-making. Some schools are so short of even these essentials that teachers have had to abandon activity work and resort to 'chalk and talk' when this is not perhaps the most suitable method of teaching. Place study also needs tracing paper, graph paper and cardboard for model-making. Paper is also needed for duplicated worksheets (made by the teacher) and a long roll of paper for time-charts. The organisation of classroom and store room are in the hands of the class teacher who should keep track of her stock and ensure that there are rules for the children to follow about this organisation.

The importance of specialised vocabulary for the learning of Place and Time has already been discussed in Chapter 3. The good teacher should plan purposefully to introduce relevant and graded words from the earliest age, building them up both on the blackboard and on work-cards, and consistently supervising the development of words for Place and Time in a special place in the children's notebooks. The use and understanding of these words can be made into quite an amusing game, and children can help each other to learn and use them properly. But it is the responsibility of the teacher to make a point of ensuring that language is a regular part of teaching. In his Dudley project John West found that historical language was all-important in historical reasoning and that the 'pilot' groups (i.e., the research groups of children) made more progress in language development than any other area of research compared with the 'control' groups (i.e., children not involved in the project).[4] The teacher should be able to address the class as a whole for oral lessons in an audible way and to use varied tones of voice when talking to individuals and groups of children. Tone of voice is very influential with young children, and positive and negative response can at times depend upon its appropriateness.

Display is still the most usual medium in the infant and junior school for recording children's work, informing others about a topic of several weeks' duration and for assessment purposes. It also stimulates enquiry and can be a most helpful teaching aid. Most colleges of education have been very much aware of this and art departments have trained students well in this respect. Although children should be trained from an early age to help with displaying their work, and eventually organise it themselves in the upper junior school, it falls to the class teacher to facilitate this, with artistic taste. A most helpful book by Ruth Phelps, *Display in the Classroom*,[5] covers two and three-dimensional displays as well as addresses to contact for suitable charts and objects to display.

Thus the good teacher as a first order resource cannot be overestimated. As Michael Pollard comments in his very valuable book *A Handbook of Resources in the Primary School*,[6] the hard-pressed teacher needs much more technical assistance with preparing and caring for resources and for mounting displays. Until there is technical assistance or teaching 'aid' Place and Time will not be adequately taught. In his extremely interesting enquiry into the teaching of History in four top primary classes, Paul Noble, himself a headmaster of a primary school, describes the teacher as all-important — 'the teacher's knowledge and enthusiasm is certainly a major resource'.[7]

Maps and Time-lines

The basic elements of both maps and sequence (time)-lines for children aged 5 to 9 is diagrammatic. Understanding Place and Time starts from plans and the concept of space in different forms. The map, sequence-line, globe, family-plan (or tree), atlas and Ordnance Survey map are all ways of recording the concept of space. Young children have to be helped very gradually to relate Place and Time to these concrete expressions of them. Therefore Place and Time have much in common here and are interdependent.

Something has already been said about how to use maps and sequence-lines in Chapter 3, and I am only concerned here with the resourcing of them. The most helpful publication for maps is by Simon Catling and is called *Mapwork in Primary and Middle Schools*.[8] This is concerned with research into children's map ability (J. Goodrow, *Children's Drawing* Fontana/Open Books, 1977, Chapter 5); with references for teachers (*The Use of Maps in Schools*, Derbyshire County Council, 1979; 'Merry Go Round', 'Getting about', *Teachers Notes*, BBC-TV, 1981; and M.J. Storm's 'Map games and stories' in *Junior Education*, July 1977, pp. 26-7); with references to books for class use by children and for libraries (*Maps of Many Lands*, Macdonald, 1974); and with references to additional resources (such as globes). Simon

Catling pays particular attention to the resources needed by infant and lower junior children.

Infants can first begin to understand routes and distance from stories about children and animals making journeys, which should be built up on the blackboard by a single line with arrows and places/buildings mentioned in the story. Such a story is *Travels of Oggy*[9] by Ann Lawrence. Oggy is a hedgehog who goes in search of the family in whose backyard he lived when they moved house. On his way he meets other animals who explain the new environment he is meeting and even tell him of lands beyond the seas. Children of 5 and 6 will encounter types of maps in their everyday life such as street signs (particularly motorway signs), the underground map and postcard maps sent by friends. 5-year-olds make picture-plans of their own homes and depict other areas such as a swimming-pool or playground, in a plan looked down from above. Children in nursery schools also use plastic playmats which can be bought in the form of a simple map.

From story an advance is made when 6 to 7-year-olds make plans of their desk top with books and pencils on it. From this they make plans of their own classrooms and later of the school's playground. In the 7 to 9 age-range a step forward is made when journeys from home to school are traced, and the route taken on a walk round the local area, in environmental work.[10] Obviously these plans cannot be bought commercially and the teacher should make her own initial examples on paper or blackboard, duplicate copies of some features for children to complete and encourage them to draw their own, eventually using rulers for straight lines. As these plans must be very simple, the large plan is not time-consuming in preparation and most teachers find no difficulty in making them.

In the later infant years children are fascinated by globes, large and small, and often wish to have one as a present. The use of a globe is a big step forward from first plans and needs some introduction by the teacher. It is useful for teaching about distant lands as well as direction and points of the compass. The most helpful addresses for globes suitable for our age-group are — E.J. Arnold, Butterley Street, Leeds LS10 1AX and J. Galt and Co. Ltd, Brookfield Road, Cheadle, Cheshire. Both these firms also supply playmats, depicting a street, a farm or a roadway.

Alongside the globe, simple atlases can be introduced and many suitable first atlases have been published. Some examples are to be found in the Books section of this chapter. Some of these are disposable, which has to be considered carefully when money is scarce, and most are intended for children of 7 years upwards. Some include lands outside Britain but most are of the British Isles. The detail in an atlas means that each child needs his own for class lessons, though a set of twelve is useful for reference even if proper study of an atlas is not undertaken before 9 years of age. A full list of publishers of atlases is given in Simon Catling's bibliographic notes, already discussed.

Younger juniors should be using large-scale OS maps by the time they reach 9. The largest one is 1:1250 scale maps (about 50″ to the mile) and the next largest is 1:2500 (about 25″ to the mile). The larger-scale shows more detail and covers a smaller area, so these are the maps to start work on with 7-year-olds. They cost from £5-7 each so it may be necessary to photocopy certain areas to make A4 size maps if the LEA has permission from the Ordnance Survey to do this, as in the case of ILEA. Schools are allowed 25 per cent discount on larger maps if ordered on a special form from: OS Department, 32 Romsey Road, Maybush, Southampton, SO9 4DH. Many local planning authorities also allow schools to use their maps.[11]

Teachers of Time in the early years receive less help from professional educators than teachers of Place. This may be influenced by the taboo put on the understanding of the concept of Time in young children by past research workers. John West has found in his larger-scale research that the youngest children can be taught the sequence of a few selected events, regardless of dates, which depend upon a developed number sense.[12] As a result of the seeming lack of need for time-lines and charts, few publishers provide commercial resources simple enough for 5 to 9-year-olds. Ladybird has produced a family-tree-type pictorial chart of English Kings and Queens which could be used by lower juniors as a reference source when they have already been taught part of English History. In this case, the chart looks upon time vertically rather than horizontally.

The most useful sequence-lines are those made by the teacher, in the first place for the children, and later by the children themselves. Examples of several of these are shown in Chapter 3 but the essence of them is a straight horizontal line divided by notches, with a minimum of dates (if any) above the line, and events or names below the line in the correct sequence. This can be tailor-made for the topic on a larger class line, showing the sequence of all topics studied in the year, put at the back of the classroom or round it. If the line is deep enough children can make relevant pictures and fasten them on the line at the appropriate places. John West advocates a rope instead of a line on paper as objects can be hung on this and it can easily be used again. Even if the teacher makes a class time-line for teaching purposes, each child should have his or her own copy on the middle page spread of their Time note-book for the year. Some teachers and children think vertically in time and can teach and learn better from a vertical line or chart. This leaves more room for writing names and the occasional date but is impossible to have one round the classroom. Paul Noble gives an excellent example of a vertical line in his pamphlet *Time Sense*.[13] This is used to learn family history, going back to great-great-grandparents, and taking in 105 years. Vertical or horizontal lines are both satisfactory but the school policy should decide on one or the other for the whole school, and also preferably the next school to be attended by the children.

Family plans or 'trees' come into this diagrammatic category as a resource. In the same way as lines, they can be arranged horizontally (with the more recent generation on the far right) or vertically (with the most recent generation at the bottom of the page). Infants cannot usually cope with more than three generations, including their own, but lower juniors can build up four to six generations, whether their own or long ago. Approximate dates can be added to the generations. An example of a horizontal family plan for 6-year-olds, using boxes for names, is shown in Chapter 3 (Figure 3.12). Family-trees are a natural way to teach Time without being encumbered by dates. They are best made for a specific piece of work, but can be used again if the topic is repeated.

Plans, maps and time-lines are basic ingredients for the study of Place and Time at any level. They come after the teacher in importance as a resource and fortunately are comparatively cheap and easy to make.

Illustrations, Photographs and Models

Slides, film-strips and the overhead projector seem to have replaced large pictures, plans and maps as teaching aids. Yet the simplicity of a large visual aid which all the class can see and which is independent of mechanical aids has much to recommend it. It is better to cover them with transparent film or to strengthen them in some way before use, as constant display can play havoc with the edges of the picture. Storage also really needs a plan press unless the pictures are rolled or kept in a drawer.

Large pictures can come from several sources. The most usual is from commercial publishers such as Pictorial Charts Education Trust[14] or Macmillan.[15] In Chapter 6 I show the valuable help gained from Pictorial Charts in their plan of the work of The Medieval Peasant; this is simple enough for 6 to 9-year-old children. Their pictures of the costume worn by the different classes of medieval England are also useful, though perhaps too highly-coloured to represent the dyes available in medieval times. They also have small charts in colour and black-and-white photographs. Some of the charts are too involved for younger children but certain items can be cut out of the chart and mounted on coloured paper with the teachers' understandable handwriting explaining it. Macmillan have published large History Class Pictures relating to British History for many years. Although again too highly-coloured they are comprehensive, dynamic in presentation and provide a starting point for class discussion.

Large commercially-produced posters may also be bought from museums and the gift shops of stately homes. Merseyside County Museum sells a most arresting poster of Liverpool overhead railway showing the docks and the railway in the late nineteenth and early twentieth centuries. The National Portrait Gallery sells large pictures of national personalities such as Richard III, the More Family Group and Elizabeth I which have the additional advantage of being original source material painted by Old Masters, rather than modern artists' reconstructions. The South Kensington Science Museum also sells accurate diagrammatic posters such as one of naval ship-building in the late seventeenth century. The Tower of London is a tremendous help to schools outside the metropolis as well as those within it. It sells large coloured photographs of the Tower now and plans of the buildings. Since the Tower comes into so much national history these aids are of great general use. I was helped by them in my teaching of Unit III, The Peasants' Revolt (see Chapter 6).

Other commercial firms and charitable agencies are often happy to give large pictures and posters to schools as propaganda for their sales. Roger Cracknell[16] gives an example of resources for teaching about India; some of his sources are Oxfam Education,[17] the Commonwealth Institute,[18] and the Natural Rubber Development Board,[19] and he also refers teachers to *The Development Puzzle*,[20] a source book for teaching towards the development of one world, and to *A Teacher's Handbook of Resources for Asia and Africa*,[21] published by the School of Oriental and African Studies in London. At the Liverpool Institute of Higher Education there is a specially-staffed World Development Studies Centre open every day for teachers to find resources, including posters, to help in their teaching of overseas Place. Teachers can also make use of posters from travel agencies for their Place work. The Association of Agriculture produces information on real farms at home and abroad. Special occasions, such as the Queen's Jubilee and the Royal Wedding and commemorative occasions such as the 1966 interest in the Battle of Hastings provide many useful, cheap or free posters. For example, in 1966 the Post Office gave large posters of the Bayeaux Tapestry issue of stamps to those who wanted them.

Perhaps the best form of large pictures and charts are made by teachers themselves since they are tailored to their particular children and are not too detailed. This is the only way to produce suitable sequence/time-lines and family plans, as well as plans of the classroom, school and environment for Place study. Unit I of Croxteth Hall has an example of a 'home-made' time line of the Molyneux family between the specific dates of 1882 and 1982 (see Figure 6.1). This type of large aid takes little time to make, provided one has large white cart-ridge paper and coloured magic markers. For 6-year-olds the number of items on the chart must be very few. It is also quite easy to mount the pages of large calendars on coloured paper; those as large as the TEAR FUND ones are ideal, but bank calendars are almost as good. These are genuine photographs or artists' work and are therefore of great value to children. Children's work is also of a high standard and if requested by teachers can form a valuable future resource for a topic. I still possess the pictures of highwaymen done by primary school children many years ago studying the Liverpool-Prescot-Warrington Turnpike road. This type of work provides inspiration to other children and is a good starting point for discussion.

Illustrations in books and postcards form another type of resource but they cannot be used for oral lessons with any but a very small group. Several postcards can be put onto coloured sugar paper, or preferably card, and leading questions about them written onto the paper for individuals and groups of children to use and answer. This is a good test of how one has taught interpretation of pictures. Even the youngest children can 'read' the illustrations in books intended for older children. Publishers are also now providing books on Place and Time topics for very young children. *Visiting a Museum* by Althea[22] is an excellent example of a good series for 7 to 9-year-old children to read, and younger children to use as picture books.

The most unlikely materials present themselves as pictures. I have found illustrated tea-towels most helpful when nothing else exists. They are easy to carry and fold without wear and tear as well as being easy to fasten up in the most awkward places. For Unit I on Croxteth

Hall, no large picture of the Hall existed, so I used a tea-towel of the Queen Anne west front, upon which the class teacher based the children's collage work (Figure 4.2). In the same way I recently found a tea-towel of The Apprentice House at Quarry Bank Mill, Styal, depicting the different rooms on the three floors of the house, with figures of apprentices helping to lay tables and going to bed. The actual Apprentice House is still standing at Quarry Bank Mill. Additional interest arises from the fact that the cotton of the tea-towel is woven at the cotton mill today.

Photographs have a particularly important part to play in the teaching of Place and are also invaluable in the study of Time during the last 150 years. They are very important for the local study of an area as

Figure 4.2: Queen Anne Front, Croxteth Hall

well as for learning about distant lands. The ILEA pamphlet gives a page to the resource bank of local pictures built up by Lucas Vale School, Deptford.[23] This consists of photographs of houses, shops and other buildings and such celebrities as The Cutty Sark, and the Queen's House, Greenwich. It also includes photographs of the area in earlier days. If children become used to looking at photographs of their own area and finding the places on a large-scale OS map, much good work will have been done by the time they are 9. There are also books of photographs of big cities published by Holmes McDougall in a series called 'This is Your Region'.[24] Aerial photography is a further use of photographs in the study of Place. The ILEA pamphlet[25] distinguishes between vertical photographs taken immediately above the area, which are particularly useful to younger children, if large enough and taking in a small area, and oblique photographs, which are taken to show the area at an angle and are therefore more like a picture and more understandable for older children who have already studied diagrams and vertical photographs. If a primary school can afford a very large local vertical aerial photograph for the entrance-hall, children of all ages are constantly referring to it (a 5' square photograph costs approximately £80).

The final resource in this section of the chapter is models. These are best made by the children themselves, from balsa wood, polystyrene, toilet rolls and corrugated cardboard. Models of farms, houses, villages, churches and tower blocks are set off better by a painted background or a map. An example of this is shown in Figure 4.3, with map and relief interrelated. The section of the recent Geographical Association Handbook, 'Hardware Models', is very useful in showing how to make contour layer models, a diagram model of a harbour town, a model of a squatter home and a landscape model.[26] The same principles of construction apply to Time models and much help can be gained from Henry Pluckrose's *Let's Use the Locality*,[27] Alan Jamieson's *Practical History Teaching*,[28] Pamela Mays' *Why Teach History?*[29] (good on dolls) and John Fairley's *Patch History and Creativity*.[30] A summary of how these authors can help us is given in my detailed book, *History in Primary Schools*.[31] Commercial models may be bought for teaching purposes but ones made by children are better as learning aids since they have to know a great deal about how a building functions to make them. A very recent model called Big Track, a vehicle of about 1½ feet in length, can link number, place and time by teaching length, time, space and direction, as well as the language of the computer.[32] It has yet to be proved a 'must' for teachers of 5 to 9-year-old children, and it certainly cannot be made by them!

Although not a first-order resource such as the teacher, illustrations, photographs and models are a great support to teachers in providing activity for young children. They help the teacher to display her own materials for teaching and to check on how much the children have learnt. In other words, children's illustrations and models are a form of assessment for the teacher, and therefore an important resource.

Figure 4.3: Relief Modelling and Mapwork

Note: A class of 8 to 9-year-olds from Greenvale Primary School, Croydon, studied the settlement of Coulsdon during the Stone and Iron Ages, and The Roman, Saxon and Norman periods. With the help of their class teacher, Mrs Hilary Cooper and Croydon Field Studies tutor Mr Ken Maggs, they used the evidence of archaeological finds, field patterns, maps and documents. The project involved many areas of the curriculum such as Mathematics, Language, Science, Art, History and Geography. After several visits, one group made this relief model, using sheets of polystyrene and painted it to show river gravels, chalk and clay soils. They devised symbols to portray evidence from each period, illustrating how the area of settlement moved from the thin soils of the chalk to the deeper clays, made possible by the introduction of the heavier plough. Another group used potato prints of the symbols to show the settlements in relation to water courses and vegetation. The map behind the relief model shows this work (1984).

Source: *Geography in Primary Schools* (Geographical Association, 1970), p. 50.

Books

Information books suitable for children aged 5 to 9 relevant to Place and Time do not exist in profusion, in contrast with those for older children. Therefore they are not at present a helpful resource for children's activity. This is borne out by two experienced professionals. Shirley Paice, deputy head of an infant school, in a hard-hitting article 'Teaching children not to read', blames teachers and publishers for not making enough effort to provide First School children with *readable* information books.[33] She says 'But what about the non-fiction so generously provided for their instruction? Is anyone reading that? Not one!' The books are provided but they remain on the shelves in pristine splendour because they are unreadable. 'There are very few simple enough books available.' Peggy Heeks, Assistant Country Librarian for Berkshire, in a gem of a book, *Choosing and Using Books in the First School*,[34] has similar facts to disclose in Chapter 6, 'Finding the facts'. Here are a few of her many most pertinent comments: 'It is unfortunate that little quick-reference material is produced for First School readership' (p. 88); 'We could benefit from a new publishing initiative' (p. 89); and 'We must remember to include reference works and books on curricular ideas for the use of staff as well as children' (p. 89). She praises books in which the text is organised on a two-stage basis, younger children needing the pictures, captions and short accounts, with good readers taking on more detailed material. Now that 7 to 9-year-olds are undertaking topics and projects involving more use of books, there is an urgent need for this type of reading material.

Although suitable books for Place and Time are scarce there are more than one imagines. I hope that publishers will see the need to find suitable authors for more to come on the market, in spite of economic recession. *Geography in Primary Schools*, the 1970 Geographical Association publication, has a good bibliography for children and teachers. The ILEA pamphlet lists story books for children according to countries; of the fifty-three titles most were published during the last twenty years but twenty were out of print by 1981 which shows a need for reconsideration by many publishers.[35] The parallel ILEA publication for History has no such list. For the sake of quick reference I will list books suitable for children aged 5 to 9 in diagrammatic form, with comment about age-suitability and my own views; I have added date of publication where possible (see pp. 93-8). This list does not include Macdonalds' Starters, which are well-known to teachers, nor is it exhaustive even in 1983. From it we can see that more suitable books have been published for Time than Place, but the latter has a greater variety of other resources to use. This accounts for the greater importance of books to Time study in The Pyramid of Resources (Figure 4.1). Historical fiction has been discussed in Chapter 3 and references made there to bibliographies; therefore these are not included in the list.

Local Environment, Field Work and Visits

After the teacher, the most important resource for the study of Place is maps. This is closely linked with field work, going out of school or using the local environment in some way. In fact, maps and field work are interdependent. No geographers believe that Place can be understood without the first-hand experience of field work, for which the use of maps is essential. Time study also draws on work outside school, though not quite so essentially, unless a local study is being undertaken.

Reference to Chapter 3 shows at what stage specialists have thought it appropriate to undertake a local study; on these occasions the teacher should plan her field work/visit first and then prepare sessions in school, both before and after the visit. This is particularly important in a large school, in which several classes need to go to the same place, and it is hoped where Place and Time are the organisational responsibility of one teacher. For infants, this often takes the form of going into the school playground to study weather, a walk in the country involving the study of water, the earth itself or a farm. Infants can also study a small portion of the nearby street, as Stephen Scoffham has shown in his very practical work.[36] A school situated in a seaside resort might also study a portion of the seashore with children aged 5 to 7. Children of this age should be able to look forward to half a day or a day's work twice a year in another locality forming an integral part of their work. This might involve Place and Time or Place or Time according to the scheme of work. Wolverhampton teachers are very fortunate in having a field study centre for nursery and infant children, opened in 1977 at the instigation of Margaret West, the Infant Adviser. In her account 'Kingswood', already referred to in Chapter 3, Mrs West speaks of this as a 'language centre' as well as a field centre, since all the new experiences the children have during their stay at Kingswood are discussed, recorded and even dramatised. The Time element is also catered for at Kingswood, as Mrs. West shows.[37]

Lower juniors can obviously undertake more ambitious field work

Books and Packs on Place Suitable for Children 5 to 9

TB = textbook series, P = pack, R = reference, A = activity

Author	Date of publication	Title	Publisher	Age-range	Type	Comments
Althea	1980	*Going on a Train*	Dinosaur	5-7	R	Introduction to railway system
Angel H.	1980	*Life on the Seashore*	Macmillan	5-9	R	Index and glossary
BEANS Series	1983	e.g., *Arab Village, Boy in Bangladesh, Sakina in India*	A. and C. Black	6-9	R	Information books, excellent, hard-backed, beautifully-presented, right size
Blackford S. (ed.)	1979	*Let's Investigate...* (Rivers, Sky, Space, Water, Rubbish)	Blackie	7-9	R	
Brook J.		*Around the Clock*	Heinemann	5-9	R	Day on the farm showing clockfaces
Catling S., Firth T. and Rowbotham, D.	1981	*Outset Geography* 1 and 2	Oliver and Boyd	7-9	TB	Excellent in all ways, teacher's guide, spirit master
Cattell, T.		*This Earth* 1 and 2	Arnold	6-9	TB	Basic physical geography, strip cartoon
Crombie I.	1968	*My Home Workbook*	Longman	5-7	A	To be used for revision when homes over world taught

Books and Packs on Place Suitable for Children 5 to 9 (Continued)

Author	Date of publication	Title	Publisher	Age-range	Type	Comments
Edward, T.		*Round the World with Teddy Edward*	Longman	6-9	R	First atlas and geography book by TV personality
Elliott, G.	1980	*Oxford New Geography for Juniors 1 and 2*	OUP	7-9	TB	Good photographs and activity, highly-coloured pictures
Jackman, L.		*Exploring the Park*	Evans	5-9	R	Excellent photographs
Lawrence, A.	1976	*Travels of Oggy*	Pan	5-7	R	Wanderings of a hedgehog from home
Leedham, J.	1973-8	*Reading Routes: Blue Box*	Longmans	6-10	P	Large-scale pack of folders, workcards, teacher's book, cassette on multi-cultural lines
Lines, C.J and Bolwell	1968	*Understanding your Environment 1, 2 and 4*	Ginn	6-9	TB	Very good, sensible and clear
Peacock, F.	1974	*Let's Go to the Railway Station*	F. Watts	5-7	R	Coloured photographs, large type-face
Pluckrose, H.	1975	*Things Up and Down*	F. Watts	5-9	R	Black-and-white photographs, brief text

Books and Packs on Place Suitable for Children 5 to 9 (Continued)

Author	Date of publication	Title	Publisher	Age-range	Type	Comments
Renwick, M. and Pick, B.	1979	*Going Places* 1 and 2	Nelson	6-8	TB	Good activity, pictures garish, spoilt by comic Noodle
Taylor, J. and Ingelby, T.	1974	*Maps for Mandy and Mark*	Longman	5-8	R	Journey of two children using maps

Books and Packs on Time Suitable for Children 5 to 9

Author	Date of publication	Title	Publisher	Age-range	Type	Comments
Allen, K.S.		*Transporting Goods*	F. Watts	5-9	R	Bold type for key words
Althea	1974	*A Visit to Canterbury Cathedral,*	Dinosaur	7-9	R	Cheap, small books, very clear illustrations on every page, most attractive
		Visiting a Museum	"	5-7	R	
	1976	*Castle Life*	"	5-7	R	
Bennett, L. and Simmons, J.	1978	*Children Making Books*	A. and C. Black	5-9	Modelling	
Booth, C.	1982	*Ships*	Heinemann	7-9	R	
Bowyer, C.		*Houses and Homes*	Usborne	5-9	R	Picture-strip form

Books and Packs on Time Suitable for Children 5 to 9 (Continued)

Author	Date of publication	Title	Publisher	Age-range	Type	Comments
Burrell, R.	1980	*Oxford Junior History* 1 and 2	OUP	7-9	TB	Clear chronological text linked to *History Long Ago* (BBC radio), very popular, garish illustrations
Chisholm, J. and Gee, R.	1983	*Usborne First History* (How Children Lived)	Usborne	6-9	R	Coloured pictures with labels
Corfe, T. (ed.)	1976 onwards	*History First*	CUP	7-9	PR	Small books, workcards, wall pictures, teacher's guide, spirit duplicator masters
Eddershaw, D.		*Homes*	Nelson	5-9	R	Two-level text for varying readers
Herbert, H.	1980	*Buildings with Character Painting Book*	Dinosaur	5-7	A	See other Dinosaur comments
	1981	*The Old Fashioned Nursery Painting Book*	"	5-7	A	
Middleton, H. (ed.)	1984	*Living in the Past*	Blackwell	7-9	TB	Lively presentation, clear type, varied illustrations
Middleton, G. and Mitchell, R. (eds)	1968 onwards	*Focus on History*	Longman	6-9	TB and R	Excellent black-and-white photographs and clear text (bold type) in chronological survey of English History, very popular

Books and Packs on Time Suitable for Children 5 to 9 (Continued)

Author	Date of publication	Title	Publisher	Age-range	Type	Comments
Moss, P.	1978-9	*History Scene*	Hart-Davis	7-10	TB and R	Comic strip type series, spirit duplicator master
Pienkowski, J.	1982	First Concepts Books: *Time, Shape, Numbers, Homes*	Heinemann	5-7	R	Small, hard-backed colourful picture books, rather expensive
Platts, J.	1972	*History Resource Library*	Macmillan	7-10	A	Teachers' guide, spirit duplicator pictures, model-making books
		Active History	"	7-10	A	
Purkis, S.	1981	*Into the Past 1900* (6 books)	Longman	5-9	R	Photographs of social life of ordinary people of 1900, excellent, very popular
Rice, P.	1972	*The Clothes Children Wore*	Dinosaur	7-9	R	See other Dinosaur comments
	1973	*The Buildings People Lived In*	"	7-9	R	
Sauvain, P.	1980 onwards	*The Story of Britain*	Macmillan	7-9	TB	Chronological series, highly-coloured illustrations
		Imagining the Past, e.g., *A Tudor Mansion, The Victorian Seaside*	"	7-10	A	
Smith, D. and Newton, D.	1971-2	In History: *Schools*	Schofield and Sim	5-9	R	Coloured illustrations, brief text

Books and Packs on Time Suitable for Children 5 to 9 (Continued)

Author	Date of publication	Title	Publisher	Age-range	Type	Comments
Wagstaff, S. (ed.)	1978 onwards	People Around Us: *Families, Friends* and *Work*	A. and C. Black	6-9	P	Very popular, multi-racial, excellent illustrations, teacher's guide, spirit masters, photographs
Waplington, A. (ed.)	1981 onwards	*History Around You* 1 and 2	Oliver and Boyd	7-9	TB	Concentric approach using themes in widening local setting, linked to Granada TV series
Various authors	1979	BEANS: *Jubilee Terrace, The Blacksmith's House*	A. and C. Black	6-9	R	See comments on Place BEANS
Various authors		Junior Reference Books: *Home Sweet Home* *Going to School* *Stars and Space* *Victorian Children* *Wartime Children*	A. and C. Black	8-10	R	Excellent illustrations, text
Various authors	1981-2	Activity Books: *Farming through the Ages* *Animals through the Ages* *Ancient Egyptians* *Toys through the Ages* *Our Town* *My First Seven Years*	CUP	6-9	A	Mainly activity, some words and writing

for longer periods, further away from school. Again, reference should be made to the schemes of work in Chapter 3, since planning of the number of visits and type of work depends upon that as well as the age-range of the school. Presuming that these children, as infants, will have studied nearby sites and that as older juniors they should be enjoying at least one residential visit far away from school, this period could concentrate on more demanding day visits. These might involve buildings interesting from the point of view of the materials from which they are built, and also because of architecture and past history. It might also involve a church,[38] a longer length of street, the centre of a village, a canal, a meandering river or even part of a small mill. Again it is sensible to consider such visits before deciding on a scheme, since they must form an integral part of the syllabus and be prepared for and resourced, in order to be repeated from year to year. This is a good age-range to involve in the study of transport facilities if safety is planned carefully. Buses, trains, aeroplanes, cars and lorries are resources for traffic-counts, as well as timetables and maps. If possible, lower juniors should be taken on field work each term; these six occasions in the 7 to 9 age period should cover as varied places and times as possible. If local study has a particularly large share in the scheme of work, more visits should be made.

Orienteering, a new 'sport', is having a tremendous popularity, especially in Scotland. This happy combination of physical exercise, use of maps and freedom from 'team games' (inappropriate for most 5 to 9 age children) can be started by children round the classroom, the playground and part of the local park. Using a simple map, each child finds his or her way round a predetermined course and punches a hole in paper hanging at certain points. This can be done walking or running and can be competitive or non-competitive as the teacher thinks fit.[39]

Place visits have usually been called 'field work' and conducted in the open air. Time visits are also called 'field work' and can be conducted outside too; they can also take place inside a building. Children aged 5 to 9 look at a stately home as a large and beautiful home of the past, as much to find out about the family which lived in it for generations (comparison with their own family homes) and to look at servants' quarters, as to study the building. In fact, I have found outside work (e.g., architecture) on the whole inappropriate with such young children. It is also necessary to limit activity within the house and study two or three rooms thoroughly. (See Unit I, Croxteth Hall in Chapter 6.) Churches are usually too 'busy' for infants unless they are small Saxon buildings (e.g., Bradford-on-Avon) or the small chapel of a stately home (e.g., that at Haddon Hall, Derbyshire). Cathedrals and large civic buildings (such as town halls) are too vast for comprehension in this age-range and to look at part of them would be pointless.

Perhaps the easiest way to bring the past alive to young children in a concrete form is to make good use of museums which have been modernised during the last twenty years. Unlike many other institutions they now have a professional education service catering for infants as well as older children. Such rapid strides have been made by the Museum Education Service that it would be impossible to do justice to them. So I shall merely consider specific museums I have found particularly useful when teaching children aged 5 to 9, from the point of view of their publications as well as their exhibits. Many others have been described by Molly Harrison,[40] Barbara Winstanley[41] and John Fairley,[42] in more specialised books.

Since its severe bombing in 1940 Merseyside County Museum has given itself a 'new look' from every point of view. As a large museum its exhibits cover many aspects of Place and Time over the last fifteen years. The Transport Gallery, housing some of the Liverpool-Manchester railway carriages and many impressive coaches, has provided a one-room base for young children. In studying the history of Liverpool with 6-year-olds I found great use was made of these large (at first frightening) vehicles, from observation as well as from the labels on them. This museum also has a Liverpool Gallery in which old streets are portrayed, as they are in the Castle Museum at York and the Abbey Museum at Kirkstall, near Leeds. Young children in the safety of the museum can gain better understanding of an old street with its buildings, shops, people (in costume), cobbles and sedan chairs, than they can 'in the field'. This museum also provides excellent worksheets for children. A particularly good one is 'The Journey', that of Elizabeth Wallace and her father from Liverpool to Manchester on the new Liverpool-Manchester railway in 1830; this involves museum exhibits, activity work and the story of a small girl as well.

London children are well-off for resources in this respect. I will mention three particularly relevant museums, the Geffrye Museum at Shoreditch, the Museum of Childhood at Bethnal Green and the Museum of London, near St Paul's Cathedral. For many years the Geffrye Museum has catered extensively for the education of children in relation to the past. It consists of English period rooms in which children can observe, sketch and complete worksheets. The Bethnal Green Museum of Childhood specialises in children's toys through the ages and also exhibits costumes, as well as providing lessons in many forms of art, including puppetry. In the same way as the Geffrye Museum it is quite unique in its specialism, and when there was a threat recently to its existence there was a public outcry, in the press and in educational circles. It is ideal for the 5 to 9 age-range. The Museum of London has many spaces devoted to the chronological display of London's history. Its spiral guide book is easy to handle and contains two colourfully-illustrated pages for each century, starting from the present. This booklet is so well presented that most 7 to 9-year-olds and some 6 to 7-year-olds could usefully concentrate on one page and museum area.

Most parts of these museums are suitable for our age-range but there are parts of other musuems which also fall into this category. The British Museum in London, well known for its exhibits of ancient civilizations, has recently published a well-constructed Activity Book on *The Romans* to match the popular *Watch* television series on BBC 2. It consists of black and white sketches of Roman life to be completed and coloured (not much indication of what colours) and many sensible activities. Let us hope that this attractive publication encourages 5 to 9-year-olds to be constant visitors to the BM in adult life. The Grosvenor Museum at Chester has one very suitable room for young children on Roman Chester, guarded by the life-size model of a Roman soldier, complete with armour, spear and shield. The amazing Singleton Open Air Museum near Chichester, set on a large campus, provides the sight of, and entry to, real medieval buildings. The museum publishes a *Museum Teaching Kit* including an excellent *Handbook for School Teachers* by Kim Leslie. In this we have a glorious example of Place and Time 'all in one go' as genuine evidence is there to see, touch and feel.

Closely connected with museum visits is the use of artefacts, or old objects, in teaching young children. These are understandable evidence for 5 to 9-year-olds. Museums often lend objects or provide handling sessions in museum classes. But there are other ways to find old objects, too. Teachers and children can bring their own, after a first session with borrowed museum artefacts, and put them in order of 'oldness' after handling and discussion. What makes an object 'old' to 6-year-olds? Is it the battered appearance, or a date on it, or because it looks unusual? This can lead to sequencing objects on a coloured tape time-line, with no actual dates, on the floor. Artefacts are outstanding genuine resources for teaching Time to almost any age. No wonder archaeology is becoming a popular subject in primary schools.[43]

The need for children to have concrete experience for a real understanding of the past is satisfied by the appropriate use of the local environment, museums and artefacts. They can be talked about and listened about as well as written about. They can even be dug up, as happened recently in one Nottingham primary school playground, quite by chance!

Hardware: Slides, Filmstrips, Films, Tapes, Discs

These resources depend upon the effective functioning of slide-viewers for individual children and film-strip, slide and cine-projectors and tape-recorders for individual, group and class work. More teachers would use them if their classrooms 'blacked out' effectively and they did not have to change to another room. They also need the help of a technician. Teachers usually need to use this type of resource for a small part of the lesson; they should use six slides intensively rather than twenty superficially.

Many outside agencies sell or rent slides of other countries to schools, possibly for propaganda purposes. For example, VCOAD has slides of town and village life in Northern Ghana. Many excellent colour slides from original manuscripts and pictures are produced by several agencies for the study of Time. Longman have sets of slides to accompany their 'Then and There' series and these can be used with younger children. Reading slides is as important as reading pictures, as John West has shown in his research. There are few suitable Time films but many short Place films for younger children, again obtainable from charitable organisations such as Oxfam and Christian Aid.[44]

Tape-recordings can be made by the teacher reading important short extracts from contemporary sources. Children can listen to these as evidence for a particular topic with questions on a workcard to answer from the tape. A fruitful discussion of Time as a concept could arise from the tape-recording of the following poem written by David Millington of Padgate C of E Primary School, Warrington.[45] This could be read by a boy of 9 and tape-recorded:

What is Time?

Is time what the hands on a clock tell?
Time you can't touch or feel or smell.
Time is a century and time is a second
Time is a minute and time is a decade.
Time is the vast array of years.

Times of happiness, times of tears.
The past was when the world was begun,
The world was created and so was the sun,
The present is now, when ever that be;
Wherever we are, you and me,
No-one knows what the future brings,
Space-age rockets and all kinds of things,
For years and years and years and years,
Time has brought hopes and time has brought fears.

Discs are useful in producing suitable music to create atmospheres for role-playing. For example, Elizabethan madrigals could accompany work on Elizabeth I's Court, or Church music could accompany Becket's murder in Canterbury Cathedral. Industrial folk songs are a good background to industrial unrest in the eighteenth and nineteenth centuries.

These are not regularly-used resources, but they bring variety to the classroom in their proper place. Much help can be gained in buying these resources from *Treasure Chest for Teachers* and from publishers' catalogues.

BBC and other TV Programmes

These programmes are an invaluable resource leading to activity for children if used sensibly. The time spent on their preparation, as with the pamphlets for teachers and pupils, is considerable, and the quality of the result is outstanding. This standard is rarely reached by individual teachers and many programmes have become regular favourites. The use of video recorders and video cassettes has led to greater use of programmes as timing has not presented such a problem. The programmes are publicised much earlier than they used to be and pamphlets can now be obtained in good time for advance preparation. This has also meant that teachers can adapt programmes to their own classes and relate them more purposefully to their schemes of work. At the time of writing, I am helping a teacher of 6-year-olds to prepare a BBC *Watch* programme for the Spring term of 1984, concerned with Robin Hood, Life in a Castle and Houses.

The 5 to 9 age-range is provided for mainly by integrated programmes though some of the 8 to 13 programmes can be adapted. The very popular *Watch* programme has topics suitable for both Place and

Time. One of these in May 1983 was concerned with 'Coastal Indians in North America' and was excellently presented. It started with 'What can you remember?' which showed a concern with continuity, and included the making of totem poles by an Indian craftsman, a classroom showing infants at work on the programme, and a large globe showing the areas where different types of Indians lived. *Zigzag* is another suitable programme, aimed more at the 8 to 9 age-range. In the Autumn of 1983 it was concerned with the Normans and proved very popular with many schools. *Movement and Drama*, intended for 7 to 9-year-olds was also concerned with Saxons and Normans, and was presented in Autumn 1983. In the same term, *My World*, for 4 to 6-year-olds, included some Place topics, such as 'Shopping Trip', 'My Town', 'Moving Home' and 'A Day Out'. *Stop, Look and Listen*, an Environmental Studies programme for 6-year-olds and upwards, has a Series A and a Series B and is concerned with particular jobs people do, such as 'Coalman', 'Dustmen' and 'Market Stall Holder'.

It is worthwhile for the teacher to view programmes intended for 8 to 11-year-olds, as many parts of them can be used for 8 to 9-year-olds. For example, *How We Used to Live*, from Victorian times to the 1950s, has been a much-used programme from Yorkshire Television, and should be tried out if this period is to be covered, though it may prove too difficult. Granada's *History Around You*, now also linked with a textbook series of the same name published by Oliver and Boyd, is concerned with local history, and very clearly led by Allan Waplington, the editor of the textbook series.

The ILEA has produced a programme called *Where We Live*, consisting of fifteen programmes on colour video cassettes, for children of 6 to 8.[46] It is very directly concerned with Place. Some of the programmes are 'Let's Go Shopping', 'Trains', and 'The Changing Years'. The Teachers' Book is very helpful about work in the classroom and outside school, as well as providing a full bibliography for children and teachers. It is not particularly limited to the London area, and is well worth experimenting with for local study.

Sound and vision programmes are a tremendous help and inspiration for non-specialist teachers. It is easy to let the programmes dictate your scheme of work but care can help teachers to use selected programmes to fit their own schemes.[47]

Resources Outside the School

In addition to field work and visits to museums there are agencies to help teachers of young children with Place and Time, beyond the professional organisations. The Geographical Association, with headquarters in Sheffield,[48] is particularly aware of the needs of this age-range and has published much invaluable material, often listed in this book. The Historical Association is just beginning to be helpful and will soon publish a pamphlet specifically for Primary School teachers.[49] The Schools Council has not catered for Time in any of its projects before the age of 8, though *Place, Time and Society*, intended for Middle School children can be adapted for 7 to 9-year-olds.[50] *Environmental Studies 5-13* has helped the local study element of both Place and Time. Since the 1978 HMI Report, many enthusiastic but overworked LEA Advisers and some Advisory Teachers and remaining Wardens of Teachers' Centres are making gallant efforts to run in-service courses and publish guidelines for their own teachers. Unfortunately, pressures in school are preventing teachers from taking full advantage of these courses. Teachers' Centres such as the ILEA Clapham History and Social Science Centre, Dudley LEA Resources Centre[51] and Merton Teachers' Centre are providing invaluable help in materials for their teachers. But there are not enough of these go-ahead LEAs to encourage teachers to branch out on new schemes of work requiring them to learn new information.

Record offices are always willing to help teachers in providing suitable documents for photo-copying for school use. The most outstanding help has come so far from Kent Record Office, with its folders edited by Teacher Adviser Margaret Phillips. The illustrative and some of the documentary material is quite suitable for use with 5 to 9-year-old children. So it can be seen that there are many resources to be obtained outside one's school if only teachers know about them and have time to sort through them for their own purposes.

Apparatus for Place Study

The study of Place has become more mathematical and scientific during the last ten to fifteen years. So the need for apparatus often found in the laboratory of a secondary school has entered the Primary School. The obvious need for sand, plasticine and clay will already be catered for in a 5 to 9 school, as also will coloured paper and a duplicator. In addition, the study of place requires the use of camera, thermometer, compass, binoculars, a tape-recorder, a mapograph and clip-boards for the older children. For earth studies a sieve is needed, as also is a magnifying glass, funnel and beakers.[52] The use of the toy truck, Big Track, has already been discussed in this chapter. Helpful advice is given also in two Geographical Association publications; one is the book edited by David Mills[53] and the other an earlier publication.[54] It is more usual, as in the case of time-lines, for home-made apparatus to be made, rather than expensive items purchased. But this home-made apparatus has to be thought about, made and stored efficiently, for general use in the school.

Family and Oral History for Time Study

This has already been discussed as a method approach in Chapter 3. It is particularly useful in the 5 to 9 age-range as the initial resource is the child's own family. Evidence for this type of Time study comes from children talking with their own families (including grandparents); old objects belonging to the family (including letters, photographs and newspaper cuttings); and in the 8 to 9 age-range some simple 'research' into the family's past. Oral history is a most suitable resource, since old people of the district can be invited to school to talk about their knowledge of it including, in many cases, of the actual school concerned. The teacher has to tread carefully in this area to avoid embarassing family situations from the past (every family has its black sheep!) and to ensure that the senior citizens invited to school have accurate knowledge, reliable memories and can relevantly answer specific questions from children. The children, too, should be advised on the questions to be asked and shown how to interview older people, particularly if they plan to tape-record the interview to play it back later. The particular attraction of family and oral history for 5 to 9-year-olds is the predominance of oral work over book-reading. Again we see that people are very valuable resources. A bank of the tape-recordings can be collected for use when old people cannot be obtained and for comparison of different interviewers. Children should learn to use the tape-recorder in small groups.

Oral work can also involve people of all ages and in all sorts of jobs. A topic on transport might involve talking to a railway driver, a bus conductor, a coach driver, a pilot or a life-boatman, all of whom will have memories of the past and will be able to describe how their work has changed over the years. This technique can apply to shopping, homes, entertainment and the circus or fair. Naturally, oral history takes us back only about sixty or seventy years, but, as has been mentioned, this is as far as many young children can comprehend. Visitors might be encouraged to help the teacher and children to construct a time-line and family-tree for themselves. Comparison of time-lines and family-trees of different visitors could be compared, with their permission. More detailed help can be obtained from Sallie Purkis' pamphlet *Oral History in Schools*.[55]

When trouble has been taken over several years to accumulate appropriate resources for a school's particular schemes, it cannot be over-emphasised that the storage and care of these materials should be in the hands of a teacher in charge of Place and Time, and the resources kept together in a particular place. By this means all teachers in the school can plan ahead to borrow suitable materials, according to their needs. Nor can it be said too often that each primary school should have some technical assistance for the repair and checking of all resources.

Notes

1. D.P. Ausubel and F.G. Robinson, *School Learning* (Holt, Rinehart and Winston, 1969), p. 492.
2. *The Rich and Poor in 19th Century Liverpool* (Merseyside County Museums Education Service, 1979).
3. *Treasure Chest for Teachers* (The Teacher Publishing Co. Ltd., Derbyshire House, Lower Street, Kettering, Northants, NN16 8BB, 1960 onwards).
4. J. West, 'Children's Awareness of the Past', unpublished PhD thesis, Keele University, 1981.
5. R. Phelps, *Display in the Classroom* (Blackwell, 1969). Other useful books in this series are: A.R. Earl, *Are the Pencils Sharpened?*; J.E. Taylor, *Materials in the Classroom*; R.H. West, *Organisation in the Classroom*.
6. M. Pollard, *A Handbook of Resources in the Primary School* (Ward Lock, 1976).
7. P.C. Noble, 'The Place of History in the Education of 11-year-olds: A Critical Evaluation of Four Schools', unpublished MEd thesis, Bristol University, 1980, p. 96.
8. S. Catling, *Mapwork in Primary and Middle Schools*, Bibliographic Notes, no. 9 (Geographical Association, 1981).
9. A. Lawrence, *Travels of Oggy* (Pan, 1976).
10. Examples of this type of work can be found in O. Garnett, *Fundamentals in School Geography* (Harrap, 1951), pp. 50, 52, 54, 55.
11. More information can be obtained from *The Study of Places in the Primary School* (ILEA Guidelines, 1981).
12. J. West, 'Time Charts', *Education 3-13*, vol. 10, no. 1 (Spring 1982); 'Thoughts on Time Charts', J.E. Blyth, *History in Primary Schools* (McGraw-Hill, 1982), pp. 120-3.

13. P. Noble, *Time-Sense* (privately published, 1981).
14. Pictorial Charts Educational Trust, 27 Kirchen Road, West Ealing, London, W13 0UD.
15. Macmillan Education Ltd., Houndmills, Basingstoke, Hants RG21 2XS.
16. J.R. Cracknell, *Teaching Geography through Topics in Primary and Middle Schools* (Geographical Association 1979), p. 56.
17. Oxfam House, 274 Banbury Road, Oxford OX2 7DZ.
18. The Commonwealth Institute, Kensington High Street, London W8.
19. The Natural Rubber Development Board, Market Buildings, Mark Lane, London EC3.
20. CWDE, Victoria Street, London SW1.
21. SOAS, Malet Street, London WC1.
22. Althea, *Visiting a Museum* (Dinosaur, 1980).
23. *The Study of Places*, p. 29.
24. Areas covered are Liverpool and Merseyside, Glasgow and the Clyde, London, Manchester, Cardiff, Birmingham and Newcastle-upon-Tyne.
25. *The Study of Places*, p. 33.
26. D. Mills (ed.), *Geographical Work in Primary and Middle Schools* (Geographical Association, 1981), pp. 89-96.
27. H. Pluckrose, *Let's Use the Locality* (Mills and Boon, 1971).
28. A. Jamieson, *Practical History Teaching* (Evans, 1971).
29. P. Mays, *Why Teach History?* (ULP, 1974).
30. J. Fairley, *Patch History and Creativity* (Longman, 1970).
31. J.E. Blyth, *History in Primary Schools* (McGraw-Hill, 1982).
32. C.V. Fox, 'Toy for Teaching', *Times Educational Supplement*, (27 May 1983).
33. S. Paice, 'Teaching children not to read', *Times Educational Supplement* (1 February 1980).
34. P. Heeks, *Choosing and Using Books in the First School* (Macmillan, 1981).
35. *The Study of Place*, p. 34.
36. S. Scoffham, *Using the School's Surroundings* (Ward Lock, 1980).
37. M. West 'Kingswood'; Blyth, pp. 101-2.
38. A. Duggan, *Look at Churches* (Hamish Hamilton, 1961).
39. I. Blomberg (Translated by J. Martland and L. Boucher), *It's Easy to Find Your Way* (Swedish Orienteering Association), copies from BOF National Office, 41 Dale Road, Matlock, Derbyshire DE4 3LT.
40. M. Harrison, *Museums* (Mills and Boon, 1973).
41. B. Winstanley, *Children and Museums* (Blackwell, 1967).
42. J. Fairley, *Patch History and Creativity* (Longman, 1970).
43. F. Dale (ed.), *Archaeology in the Primary School* (Council for British Archaeology, 1982).
44. Christian Aid, PO Box 1, London SW9.
45. From *Education in Cheshire* (Cheshire LEA, Autumn 1975).
46. *Where We Live*, Teacher's Book (ILEA, 1977).
47. *Teachers' Use of Educational Television in Infants Schools*, (1983) is a critical survey obtainable from L. Smith, School of Education, University of London, Goldsmith's College, New Cross, London SE4, for £1.00.
48. The Geographical Association, 343 Fulwood Road, Sheffield S10 3AP.
49. The Historical Association, 59a Kennington Park Road, London SE11 4JH; A. Low-Beer and J.E. Blyth, *Teaching History to Younger Children* (Historical Association, T.H. 52, 1983).
50. Blyth, *Primary Schools*, pp. 54-61.
51. J. West, 'The Development of a Local Resources Centre', *Teaching History*, vol. II, no. 7 (May 1972).

52.   H.M.E. Barber and J.Y. Hayes, *Exploring the Physical World with Children, 5 to 9* (Dent, 1973) Chapter 6.

53.   Mills (ed.), p. 23, (windvanes); p. 161 (fossils and rocks).

54.   *Teaching Geography in the Junior School* (Geographical Association, 1962) pp. 37-48.

55.   S. Purkis, *Oral History in Schools* (Oral History Society, 1980).

Part Three

ASSESSMENT AND RECORD-KEEPING

Part Three

ASSESSMENT AND RECORD-KEEPING

5 ASSESSING PLACE AND TIME

Most teachers want to check on the value of their schemes, the effectiveness of their methods of teaching, the suitability of resources used
by the children and the progress made by them. In recent years much
work has been done on accountability in Number and Language, but
Place and Time, as with all areas of topic work, particularly in the 5 to
9 age-range, have not been considered sufficiently important to evaluate. John Bentley links this inertia as regards Place to lack of planned
schemes and objectives in its teaching; he says 'It is the lack of specific
guidelines which deters evaluation' because "you cannot produce
successful evaluation of geographic learning without explicitly stated
objectives" (Kaufman, 1971, p. 27)[1] Phil Clift also links planned
schemes with record-keeping when he writes of 'the relationship between curriculum planning and record-keeping — the alpha and the
omega of the matter'.[2] In this book I have already suggested guidelines
as to the form of schemes, and skills and concepts to be taught, so it is
now more possible to formulate a practicable method of assessment
and record-keeping.

Some definitions of terms are needed to make this chapter specific
and helpful. Not much is going to be said about evaluation, since there
is a dearth of published materials for 5 to 9-year-olds in Place and Time
and there is less need to evaluate teacher-made materials. Evaluation is
concerned with checking on schemes of work, methods of approach
and effectiveness of resources. More help can be gained for both Place
and Time from my book *History in Primary Schools* which gives an
evaluation scheme for books, one for archive units and teaching kits,
and a checklist for workcards.[3] Assessment of pupils' work, our main
concern, can be done both by teachers and pupils themselves, and
suggestions for the 5 to 9 age-range will be made later. Record-keeping
is closely associated with assessment of pupils' work since children,
parents, other teachers and, eventually, other schools need a record of
the child's standard and progress in Place and Time. Assessment can
also be done informally through discussion between teachers and children; this is very valuable and leads to progress, but is not usually
recorded in detail. So evaluation is less necessary than are assessment
and record-keeping, on which I shall be concentrating.

Assessment and record-keeping have their advantages and disadvantages. When schemes of work have been thought out and are being implemented, and a whole school staff is co-operating to improve children's awareness of Place and Time, satisfaction is gained from assessing children's progress, and thinking out ways of overcoming the difficulties of those not making progress. It is also a stimulus to the children, particularly the intelligent but lazy ones, and can lead to fruitful discussion between parents and children hitherto limited to Number and Language skills. On the other hand, all assessment tends to be subjective, particularly in Place and Time. It can cause tension for less able but sensitive children who have yet another area of the curriculum in which to fail, and unless carefully planned, can cause work for the teacher who might be better employed in preparation of activities. With regard to the latter Phil Clift emphasises that 'simplicity of recording techniques appeared to be an overriding factor' in his discussions with teachers.[4]

How Shall We Assess Place and Time?

As there are more advantages in assessing children's work than not doing so, the practical question arises for the class teacher of children aged 5 to 9 — how shall we do it efficiently and quickly? As many of the skills and concepts of Place and Time are identical, I shall consider them together, adding specific needs where necessary. There are five stages:

1. To decide upon objectives to assess for Place and Time, an an objective being what a child can *do* after teaching. This is usually a practical skill, since teaching concepts cannot be assessed by the age of 9, and probably not by the age of 11.
2. To apply this list of objectives to the 5 to 7 age-range at the end of each year.
3. To apply it incidentally as one goes along, in the 7 to 9 age-range.
4. To apply it on a longer-term basis for 7 to 9-year-olds at the end of the year.
5. To decide upon a school policy for keeping records.

Let us look more closely at the desired objectives for Place and Time. I shall discuss them in order of importance. Figure 5.1 gives a Place and Time Class Profile for recording work done and the standard reached by the class as a whole. It will be discussed in more detail later

Figure 5.1: Place/Time Class Profile

Aims and Objectives	Name of teacher 7 to 8-year-olds	Name of teacher 8 to 9-year-olds
1. *Knowledge* of — local area — local history — stories of the past		
2. Understanding and use of geographical and historical *language*		
3. *Skills*: — using and making — diagrams and maps — using evidence — reading books to find information — writing paragraphs		
4. *Oral work* — tell a story — talk about a place and the past — ask questions		
5. *Empathy*: Begin to understand people and appreciate varying environments		
6. *Sequence* and time-sense, space-sense		
7. Completion of satisfactory *topic/ project*: neatness in presentation, imaginative display of work		

in this chapter, but the objectives on the left-hand side are those suitable for Place and Time. Young children should have knowledge of their local area and be able to enjoy telling stories of the past. The school must decide how far afield 'local' is, whether it is the area round the children's school and homes, or the village, town, city, county or even bigger area. Children aged 5 to 9 could only have direct experience of a small area, but could get to know about a wider area from maps, slides and descriptions. Although many Greek myths and legends are too involved and factual for this age-range[5] there are many 'heritage' stories which are not likely to be told after the junior school. For example, stories of Joan of Arc, King Arthur, Robert the Bruce and even Winston Churchill are frequently referred to in everyday life (on television, in the press, in films, plays and novels) and older children hesitate to admit their ignorance. This applies equally well to fiction. Therefore a first objective should be limited but secure knowledge. This obviously needs an agreed scheme to avoid repetition of localities and stories.

I have discussed the need for specific teaching of Place and Time vocabulary and the building up from the age of 5 of specific words used in the correct context. School policy should decide which Place/Time words are appropriate at which stage. Oral checks and later written ones should be made to ensure that they are being used correctly. At the infant stage many teachers check on specialised vocabulary by talking to children[6] and asking them to 'tell a story back', using as many of the correct words as possible. So a 'village' might be defined as a 'small number of houses in the country' and children should use the one word instead of long explanation. In the same way 'servants' exist in the nineteenth and early twentieth centuries, while 'maids' exist in the 1920s and 1930s. 'Breeches' are worn in the eighteenth century and earlier, whereas 'jeans' and 'shorts' are worn today. Teachers should be consistently checking on these differences, for good use will only be built up gradually. Short tests can be given about twice a term as checks on vocabulary learning from words built up in the children's notebooks. These tests are very enjoyable and can become quite a game, with children testing one another. There is no need to make any formal record of them. When books start to be used in earnest, vocabulary is enlarged much more rapidly, especially if children are encouraged to use dictionaries.

A third objective is the teaching of skills. One is that of finding out information, by the use of the contents, index and glossary of books. This also necessitates library reference skills which cannot be started too soon in order to avoid children only using books suggested by their teacher or those books in their own class libraries. Keith Cooper has more detailed advice about reference skills.[7] Children should also begin early the practice of reading and using maps and diagrams and learning to make their own simple maps, possibly including their route to school. This also applies to using evidence, particularly oral evidence and artefacts, which necessitates careful and accurate listening on the part of young children as well as the handling and close observation of objects. The final essential skill is that of writing a short paragraph about some place, some event or personality in time past. Into this narrative should come empathy and imagination, which can be checked by the reaction of the class when the writing is read aloud.

An objective developed from the learning of special vocabulary is that all children should be able to participate in oral work about Place and Time. They should learn to talk to the whole class, to the teacher and to their peers in small groups. These areas of the curriculum lend themselves naturally to conversation, describing visits, asking about old objects, role-playing events and discussing the way people in other lands live. This leads on to the objective of beginning to understand people by discussing them and their motives. For example my 9-year-olds got to appreciate Richard II's dilemma (Richard was 14 years old in 1381), set as he was between the peasants and his courtiers and churchmen.[8] The sympathetic understanding of Place takes the form of appreciating the environment in which one lives, however unpalatable, and learning to see differences in varying environments. City children can learn to appreciate the seashore or the country through visits, yet they can learn to see the good in their own enviroment too.

Enough has been said already in this book about encouraging children to use sequence/time-lines as soon as possible, and several examples have already been given of early lines. As a concept beyond the experience of 5 to 9-year-olds, constant practice in using lines, talking about words denoting time, and introducing time elements into discussion will gradually help this objective to be attained. The sense of space, and objects in relation to each other in space, can be demonstrated more easily, but again it is an objective only slowly gained.

All such objectives are tested when a topic or project is undertaken by a class of children. Teachers should take care to check that the objectives discussed are introduced into topic work and that this is presented neatly and attractively in preparation for detailed map work in the later stages of the junior school and in the secondary school. In all group work in topic approaches, care should be taken to know which work is done by individual children so that assessment can be made. In assessing a topic/project the teacher should ask whether the information is true, accurate and relevant; whether illustrations are appropriate and carefully executed; whether the work as a whole is well-planned and presented; and whether the individual or group has shown initiative in carrying out the topic/project. Stephen Scoffham has some helpful comments to make about appraisal of a project on urban studies in the primary school, and the Gunnings and Jack Wilson on the evaluation of topic teaching.[9]

Such objectives as discussed above must be 'matched' to the abilities and age of the children concerned, otherwise assessment has no purpose. Thus, if children aged 5 to 9 are given work too easy or too difficult, a 'mismatch' will occur. For example, if average 8-year-olds were asked to write a composition comparing Elizabeth I and Mary Queen of Scots, instead of a short account of The Armada, this would be a 'mismatch', and assessment of the compositions produced would be pointless. Dr Wynne Harlen has applied this 'mismatch' idea to science teaching, but it is also relevant for Place and Time.[10]

The second stage of assessment is to apply these objectives to the 5 to 7 age-range, for which the teacher could use the chart in Figure 5.2 as a guide. With these in mind she should look for the introduction

Figure 5.2: Place/Time Concepts and Skills as Objectives in the Infant School

Concepts	Skills
1. Age of objects and age of people	1. To observe and gain evidence from pictures, maps, plans, buildings, artefacts
2. Sequence of events	
3. Changes in time	2. To find out and use knowledge of own family as far back as possible
4. Relationship between people and events	3. To communicate by telling, drawing or making a plan or map
5. Relationship between objects in space	4. To begin to understand the point of view of others
	5. To make simple diagrams and route maps

and use of specific Place/Time vocabulary and build it up in the children's books; the sequencing of events and people (not using any dates); general interest in the past and understanding of the beginnings of evidence, (the question 'How do we know?' should constantly be asked). Children of this age can be assessed informally in three ways. The first is through small group discussions between children, with the teacher going round groups to check on the concepts and skills being developed. For example, children bringing old objects, pictures and books to school, talking about television programmes and showing curiosity about the world outside school would be fulfilling the objectives. Secondly, each child would keep a Place/Time or topic book for the year, the small group could give views on each book, and the teacher could finally decide which children should have P, T or P/T on their individual school record cards. The latter would be near the name of a child showing great interest or ability in Place and Time. This would mean the minimum of work for the teacher, who would be completing individual record cards in any case. Finally the task list given by John Foster in *Discovery Learning in the Primary School*[11] could be adapted to suit Place and Time by selecting twenty-one out of forty tasks, with the teacher using them as a guide to deciding about P, T or P/T on the record card. Figure 5.3 is an adaptation of John Foster's task list.

Figure 5.3: Place/Time Task List for Infants

---

1. Uses school library books well.
2. Understands library classification system.
3. Uses books for finding out.
4. Can tell a simple story.
5. Can read a story to a friend.
6. Knows address.
7. Can write address.
8. Shows interest in neighbourhood environment.
9. Shows interest in classroom environment.
10. Brings to school things of interest.
11. Contributes to discussion.
12. Knows days of week.
13. Knows months of year.
14. Shows interest in discovery.
15. Uses spatial terms accurately.
16. Can tell the time.
17. Has made some models (a) independently (b) with a group.
18. Knows the seasons and seasonal activities.
19. Knows the Highway Code.
20. Can name three books on class bookshelf.
21. Can answer questions on these books.

Source: J. Foster, *Discovery Learning in the Primary School* (RKP 1972) (adapted).

The third stage of assessment is to apply the objective incidentally in the 7 to 9 age-range during the year. This very much depends on the planning and activities during the year, as suggested by the findings of a group of teachers at a DES regional course on assessment. This is their conclusion: 'We are convinced that systematic planning of activities and materials for the pupils we teach is the best way of beginning to diagnose and assess what is going on in the classroom.'[12] If these are appropriate, the teacher should assess by two methods. The first is by asking the right questions in class, both 'open' and 'closed', to find out the general impression of the class as a whole, as well as very good and poor individual children. The second method is self-assessment by the children of themselves. This is advised by several educators as general asessment including Place and Time. Mary Cooper tells how her 8-year-olds wrote their own records at the end of each day. From a blackboard list the child found out what work she had done, added details about how far she had got with it and wrote down her feelings about her work and how she thought she had done it.[13] Joan Dean[14] and John Foster (pp. 79-81) have also written about how individual children keep their own records.

The fourth stage is long-term assessment for the 7 to 9 age-group at the end of each of the two years. In the first place children should assess each other's work in groups, having been trained to do this sensibly from early infant years. This could form part of an end-of-year procedure, when all Place/Time books could be collected and a whole morning or afternoon set aside for the work. The result should be comments from the group rather than grades. With the help of this group assessment, the oral questioning and children's self-assessment, the teacher should be able to assess each child's Place/Time work for the year on an A-D scale (A = excellent, B = very good, C = satisfactory and D = weak), written on each child's individual general record card in the space for Topic, Environmental Studies, Place/Time work. Those children who naturally excel at Number and Language always seem to be called 'clever' yet there are many who have a deep interest in Place and Time who receive no such accolade. Receiving D in Number and C in Language (or comments to that effect) could be offset by an A or B in Place/Time work.

The last stage of assessment is simple and efficient record-keeping, essential if assessment is to be shown over a long period. Phil Clift has emphasised that teachers need specific time in school to complete their record cards and that only 2 per cent of all LEA record cards were completed for Environmental Studies. To gain this simplicity I suggest two methods of approach. The first is the preparation of school record cards for each child, with a reasonable space for Place/Time work so that the teacher can put A, B, C, D in the space, with a comment of appreciation or the reverse. The second, in addition, or as an alternative, is the Place and Time Class Profile as in Figure 5.1. This should be completed for the class as a whole to let colleagues know what work has been done (particularly if the scheme has not been followed exactly), and also as a check on progress made by the class as a whole. Figure 5.1 shows the first two junior years but this profile could well extend into the upper junior years.

If assessment and record-keeping are to be effective, they must be quick to carry out and must not frighten children and so prevent them from doing their best. In Place and Time, assessment should not only be concerned with written work or a display, though both these methods of approach have their uses. Children should be encouraged to know that sustained interest, oral work and reading are all equally important for gaining a very good assessment. Place and Time study demand many important qualities other than those which are needed for other areas of the curriculum, and these should count towards a general assessment of children's achievement.

Notes

1.   J. Bentley, 'Evaluation in Geography' in D. Mills (ed.) *Geographical Work in Primary and Middle Schools* (Geographical Association, 1981), p. 177.

2.   P. Clift *et al.*, *Record-Keeping in Primary Schools* (Macmillan, 1981), p. 237.

3.   J.E. Blyth, *History in Primary Schools* (McGraw-Hill, 1982).

4.   Clift, p. 238.

5.   F. Saxey, *Classical Stories* (OUP, 1968) tells six famous stories simply enough for our age-range. ('Ass's Ears', 'Pegasus', 'Persephone', 'Holding Up the Sky', 'Mother Wolf', 'The Geese that Hissed').

6.   J. Tough, *Listening to Children Talking* (Ward Lock, 1976), 'the concept of appraisal', p. 32 and Part III.

7.   K. Cooper, *Evaluation, Assessment and Record-Keeping in History, Geography and Social Science* (Collins/ESL, 1976), p. 16.

8.   See Unit III, Chapter 6.

9.   S. Scoffham, *Using the School's Surroundings* (Ward Lock, 1981), Chapter 9, p. 96; S. and D. Gunning and J. Wilson, *Topic Teaching in the Primary School* (Croom Helm, 1981), 'Evaluating Children's Work', pp. 131-55.

10.   W. Harlen, 'Matching' in C. Richards (ed.) *Primary Education: Issues for the Eighties* (Black, 1980).

11.   J. Foster, *Discovery Learning in the Primary School* (RKP, 1972), pp. 77-8.

12.   *History, Geography and Social Studies in the Curriculum 5-14 – a Workshop Course on Assessment of Children's Progress*, DES Regional Course, University of Liverpool School of Education, (Autumn 1979), p. 25.

13.   M. Cooper, 'Children as Assessors', *Times Educational Supplement* (21 July 1978).

14.   J. Dean, *Recording Children's Progress* (Macmillan, 1972).

Part Four

THEORY INTO PRACTICE

Unit I: Time Unit on Croxteth Hall with 6 and 7-year-olds

I taught this historical unit of work about a local stately home in Liverpool over a period of half a term, involving two sessions a week.

The School and Children

The infant school chosen for this experiment was near the centre of Liverpool, in Wavertree, a stable working-class area. It fed a junior and a girls' secondary modern school, and all were housed in red-brick Edwardian buildings with a railed playground. Most of the children lived in well-kept terraced houses in the streets around the school. Numbers were declining, except for a large reception class. The top class had twenty-seven children in it, out of which I took ten for my experiment. All the members of staff were women, most being experienced and very competent. Space was plentiful and I was fortunate to teach my small group in a well-endowed spare room with several display boards, facilities for projecting and black-out curtains. While I taught my group about the Molyneux family and Croxteth Hall between 1882 and 1982, the class teacher developed the theme with the rest of the class, to include different types of houses, poor people in Victorian times and how they lived. She worked on friezes, books, Victorian paper plates (mock pottery) and a display of Victoriana, to offset the Queen Anne side of Croxteth Hall made by the class. Therefore in my absence the children had a stimulating, relevant curriculum which gave extra dimension to their work with me. This particular infant school very much believed in children being 'stretched' as much as possible.

Preparation of the Unit

As I had chosen to study a local stately home, material had to be gathered from many sources; no one book supplied enough detail. This involved three personal visits to the Hall, a visit to a Liverpool Education Authority Resources Centre for photocopying material, and a visit to Liverpool Record Office to consult the archivist and look for photographs and sketches. I also visited the Children's Library in the Central Library and two Branch libraries, all of which willingly lent books for the children for the period of preparation and teaching (i.e., about two months). Two visits were also paid to the school to make plans, have materials duplicated for the children and collect coloured paper to make into individual books and for mounting display material. A Teachers' Folder was bought from Croxteth Hall and proved most useful and a good basis for more reading and activities for the children. As this was an experiment, I prepared one session at a time in order to adjust future sessions to the needs of the group. The school provided me with their usual lettering of the alphabet and formation of numbers up to 5. I had to use numbers larger than five (i.e. 1882-1982), and a hundred years for the time-line, but the children did not seem to have much difficulty with these large numbers.

Content

The topic undertaken, The Molyneux Family and Croxteth Hall (Liverpool) 1882-1982, had many advantages for top infants. It was local and therefore very relevant to them. The Molyneux family is an old-established one; the French name (which the children had no difficulty in pronouncing) betokens its arrival in England with William the Conqueror in 1066. The Conqueror gave lands in the north-west to the Molyneux in return for their loyalty, the chief area being Sefton, just north of Liverpool. This family built Croxteth Hall, nearer Liverpool, in Elizabethan days (the late sixteenth century) when Liverpool Castle in the centre of the town was pulled down, and they extended the Hall to its present size as a stately home. The Hall can easily be visited, and caters well for children. One hundred years was a good length of time for children to grasp and the Victorian and Edwardian artefacts involved were fairly easily provided with the help of Merseyside Museum and Croxteth Hall. The topic also involved discussion of how people lived in a large house, their activities and leisure pursuits, and the relationship between the family and servants. Thus 6 and 7-year-olds could grasp such concepts as loyalty being linked to land, the difference between their own homes and Croxteth Hall (also involving extending a building according to the period concerned) and the difference between the leisured rich and the hard-working poor.

During the six sessions the work came to be studied under four headings:

1. The Molyneux Family 1882-1982
2. A visit to Croxteth Hall — preparation and follow-up

3. Victorian and Edwardian costume for women, men and children, including servants
4. Life at Croxteth Hall about 1900

How the Unit Was Taught

Each of the six sessions (with the exception of the visit to Croxteth Hall) lasted one hour and ten minutes, that is, the period before break in the afternoon. After this I was able to stay in the room we used, mark the work done by the children and fasten their work (photocopied or duplicated) into their Croxteth Hall books, which I had made of coloured sugar paper. During the session the children worked at tables and used the visual aids to help them, or alternatively they sat on a carpet in another part of the room to talk with me in a group about the work, discuss the illustrations and look at slides.

Session 1: The Molyneux Family, Lords Sefton. After writing their own names on the new workbooks we started on the meaning of the words 'Croxteth Hall'. This was approached in several different ways. They looked at the covers of the workbooks which I had made for the curious spelling of the words. As they were Liverpool children the district of Croxteth was already familiar to them. We also looked at the picture of the eighteenth-century side of the Hall on a linen tea-towel (bought from the Hall shop for want of any other large illustration). We also looked at a poster provided by the Hall and two early twentieth-century photographs (an aerial view of the Hall in its grounds and a sketch of the north front and main entrance). The children realised that a hall was a very large house in its own grounds, for many of them had visited other 'stately homes' both in Liverpool (the Elizabethan Speke Hall) and in other parts of the country. Thus, by looking at the words in various places and seeing the Hall from different angles, the idea of Croxteth Hall was implanted, to be further reinforced by our visit the following week.

From this initial work we passed on to the Molyneux family, who lived there from the sixteenth century to 1972 when the seventh Lord Sefton (also called an 'Earl') died and left the hall to Merseyside Corporation for the public to enjoy. This work was started with a large visual aid called Time-Line for Lord Sefton and Croxteth Hall (Figure 6.1). Each child had an A4 version of the larger one and could work from it by using a pencil or finger along the line as I talked about the dates of the hundred years under discussion and worked from the larger visual aid on the display board. This time-line, presented from left to

Figure 6.1: Time-line for Lord Sefton and Croxteth Hall

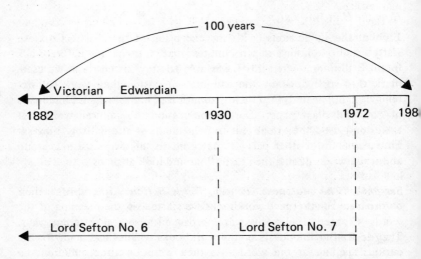

right instead of vertically seemed to cause no problems, and all knew that the 1982 of the far right was 'today' and that the 1882 of the far left was 'a long time ago'. We worked from 1975 when most of the children were born and went back to 1972, and from there back to 1930 when the seventh Lord Sefton began to own Croxteth Hall (not the duration of his life, which could have been confusing). We then moved back to 1882 when the sixth Lord Sefton, father of the seventh, was already in charge (arrow back shows this) until the time he died, in 1930. We also found out that the seventh Lord Sefton had a wife but no children, therefore it was explained that there could not be an eighth Lord Sefton, and in 1972 the Hall became the property of the Corporation. From this we also learnt that Lord Sefton's wife was called Lady Sefton, not Mrs Sefton.

The time-line also introduced discussion about 'Victorian' and 'Edwardian' and what the words mean. Some of the children already knew that Victorian was connected with Queen Victoria but they had to be told about Edward VII. The long reign of Queen Victoria and the short one of Edward VII were compared; this made them realise that Victoria was Queen far to the left, off our time-line. The adjective 'Victorian' being joined to any object or person during that reign gradually became real and proved very useful later in our work on artefacts. I omitted George V, Edward VIII, George VI and Elizabeth II on the time-line, as too confusing. The children were told that other kings reigned between Edward VII's death (actually 1910, but not marked) and the present queen.

Having talked about Croxteth Hall and the time-line we thought about the Molyneux family and related them to the Lords Sefton. We started from Christian names and surnames, which we all had, but found that none of us had 'titles', as we had never owned large amounts of land in our families for many years. We found that some of our families did not own a house and paid rent or lived with another part of our family. We then talked about Charles Windsor, Prince of Wales, and found that he had a Christian name and a surname but also a title. Thus William Molyneux was also Lord Sefton and had a title and land and was the seventh earl because his father, grandfather and four others had owned Croxteth Hall and been called Lord Sefton; they also had Molyneux as a surname. This was taught from a simple diagram on the blackboard (Figure 6.2) as well as discussion:

Figure 6.2: Blackboard Diagram for Names and Titles

Christian name	Surname	Title
Mary	Jones	————
Charles	Windsor	Prince of Wales
William	Molyneux	Lord Sefton (7th)

Each child had an A4 Molyneux coat-of-arms and one I had had coloured, on display (Figure 6.3). To understand heraldry we returned to William I who gave some loyal supporters a coat-of-arms to wear in battle as a badge and as a sign of status and approval. It usually had a complimentary phrase in Latin on it (in this case *vivere sat vincere* = to live is enough to conquer) and was made up of parts representing the family. For instance, the Molyneux arms had a coronet on it to show that Lord Sefton was an 'earl' and a peacock feather in a cap. Therefore we began to realise that the Molyneux family was no ordinary one. It had land given by the king, at least one large house, a title and a coat-of-arms.

To add to the family's importance it was given Liverpool Castle (Figure 6.4) by King Henry VI. This was in the centre of Liverpool near the River Mersey and was used to defend Liverpool against her enemies. Each child also had an A4 picture of Liverpool Castle, to be seen as a

Figure 6.3: Arms of the Sixth Earl of Sefton

Source: Teachers' Pack from Croxteth Hall, Liverpool, 1980.

large model in Croxteth Hall and there was a copy on display. We looked at the drawbridge, strong castellated walls and keep of the castle, as well as the moat full of water. This was a secure house for the Molyneux to live in and when it was pulled down the family began building an undefended home, Croxteth Hall, as England was then more peaceful. Comparison was made between Croxteth Hall and Liverpool Castle as regards safety.

So far the session had been conducted as discussion, question and answer, using pictures and the time-line. Thus the children were interested and eager to do something themselves. From my example on display and a list of colours for the coat-of-arms they used crayons to colour their own copies. Many came from their tables to look at my

Figure 6.4: Liverpool Castle

Source: *A Town under Siege: Liverpool and the Civil War, 1642-4* (Liverpool History Teaching Unit no. 3, 1978).

example more closely and most avoided crayoning over the edge of the coat-of-arms. We also talked about how to colour Liverpool Castle — grey building, green grass inside the walls, blue water in the moat and blue River Mersey with a red-sailed boat in the river. This was done another day with the class teacher as time was by this time running short.

Session 2: The Building of Croxteth Hall and Preparation for our Visit. This session started by revision of the last one with the children sitting on the carpet around me. We used the large time-line, pictures of the coat-of-arms, Liverpool Castle and Croxteth Hall and a word list built up during the previous session. Names and dates were remembered enthusiastically and well.

Two diagrammatic outline pictures were used to find out how Croxteth Hall was built. One showed the 1572 Elizabethan building, to be seen as a model at Croxteth Hall, and the 1982 present-day hall. We started from the children's own houses and their school, both built at 'one go' and the Hall, altered, extended and built over one hundred years, referring to the time-line. By counting the windows in both pictures, comparisons were made as to size. They were asked how long *ago* the first house was built (over four hundred years − an exercise in number) and which word described the present hall best, cottage, mansion, castle, palace or stately home. All these words conjured up different pictures, with references to Liverpool Castle and Buckingham Palace. Stately home was finally chosen. The second picture was four ground plans of the Hall dating from c. 1700, 1800, 1900 and today (another reference to the time-line), showing in black the parts added to the building. Points of the compass were on the diagram to show the direction in which each side of the Hall was facing. Exercises were done on direction to consolidate this work. The children were asked to imagine that they were flying in an aeroplane looking down on the Hall and watching it getting bigger and bigger. Use was made of the tea-towel and the other pictures of the Hall to find out which side the pictures showed, north, south, east or west.

Preparations for our visit to the Hall were made by imagining we were going round as we did on our visit. We then looked at a selection of slides lent by it and I asked the children questions, many of which covered material already known, such as the Molyneux coat-of-arms, Liverpool Castle and the pictures of the outside of the Hall and Croxteth Park. Looking at twelve slides from a bigger selection provided by Croxteth Hall held their attention, but more than this would have been counter-productive.

Session 3: Our Visit to Croxteth Hall, 10.00-11.30 a.m. The class teacher accompanied me on this visit with my small group of ten children, and the school chartered a mini-bus for the occasion. I had decided to concentrate on the inside of the Hall in the one-and-a-half hours, and this was as well, since the day was very windy and cold (30 April). With greater knowledge of the group than I then had, I would have looked at the Queen Anne west front and the more sober Edwardian north front through which we entered, since these two features kept appearing in our later work. As the Hall was complicated as a building, having been added to, the official guide agreed to meet us at the kitchen at 10.30 a.m. to take us to our 'classroom' for discussion and a sit-down at 11. He would have taken us on a guided tour for he knew a lot about the costume section, but we wanted to question the children, as well as inform them in our own way, as prepared beforehand at school. Unless a guide is an experienced teacher of young children, the class teacher is usually a better guide, as she can relate the visit to work in the school.

The first part of our tour was a display of pictures and models of Croxteth Hall, starting with a large coloured model of the Molyneux coat-of-arms which the children had coloured for their workbooks. Other features were landscapes of Croxteth Park in the nineteenth century and Croxteth high-rise flats today; this was a basis of comparison and contrast. A rather gruesome life-size model of a medieval hunter and his dead deer elicited horror and disapproval from the group. The model of the original 1572 Hall, already seen as a picture in school, led to much discussion and comparison. Lord and Lady Sefton's robes for their Court appearances led us to the words 'earl' and 'countess', to the House of Lords (what it is, and who attends) and to the actual materials used for the robes (white ermine fur, red velvet, gold braid etc.) The replicas of the Molyneux brasses, now closely-guarded in Sefton Church, introduced the concept of 'commemoration' and the prospect of brass-rubbing in the future. The class teacher assembled a display of brass utensils for the school entrance hall on the strength of this connection. The large model of Liverpool Castle, with its background of the River Mersey, led to great excitement and comparison with their own pictures of this original Molyneux stronghold. So few children were familiar with going into the centre of Liverpool that it was difficult to relate the castle to the present Castle Street and the Victoria Memorial on the site of the original castle. The display was completed by large photographs of the rooms of the Hall c. 1900, the heyday of social life and activity for the family.

After this display we watched a tape-slide sequence of the Hall and the family from about one hundred years ago. This number of years had already been discussed at school and seen on the children's time-lines. This sequence included the seventh earl's twenty-first birthday party, photographed on the grand steps of the Queen Anne front, and the estate agent (explanation needed) looking after the home farm, servants, parties and the additional Molyneux shooting lodge in the north of Lancashire. The only difficulty with this was our inability to stop the sequence and explain difficult concepts to the children.

The slide-tape sequence led into the display of relics of Lord Sefton as a well-known Lancashire sportsman, showing hare-coursing, cock-fights, shooting parties and, above all, the Grand National race course at Aintree which the Molyneux family patronised. The models of animals and the real guns intrigued the children, who, back in school, linked this visual presentation to a picture-making exercise. This display ended with a large photograph of the last Lord Sefton.

The cobbled courtyard was our next port of call. Here a large assembly of old carriages gave an opportunity for spotting a coach with the Molyneux coat-of-arms emblazoned on it. Work was also done later on carriages, and a visit to the Transport Gallery at the Merseyside Museum would have been a good development of this work. A wheelwright's base was used to mend the wooden and metal wheels of the carriages. Our visit to the 1920 kitchen was not as productive, as no-one is allowed to look round, and a barrier only allowed us to view, not to handle, utensils. On our way there we felt and touched an original sixteenth-century heavy doorway, and saw a parlour for the servants to use in their sparse leisure time. At this point the guide led us up the simple back stairs, used by servants, to the grand gallery and wide ornamented stairs used by the family − an obvious contrast. We passed a large display of costumes very quickly, as this was too much to take in. Then we were taken by the guide to a classroom with a table, chairs and benches.

Here I recapped on our journey so far, asked questions and explained queries put by the children. This gave us all a rest and collection of ideas before going on to the bedrooms of Lord and Lady Sefton. In this classroom, where clipboard and pencils could be provided for older children, I also prepared the children to look at the two bedrooms and private bathrooms. In the bedroom I asked questions about furniture, differences in the rooms, differences in clothes from our clothes, and the reasons for comfortable chairs and tables being in the rooms. The children were intrigued by the variety of hats in Lord Sefton's wardrobe − why did he have so many?

The rest of the time before the mini-bus returned was spent in each child selecting one tenpence purchase from the shop. The children seemed very lively at the end of the one and a half hours walking round and could possibly have done more, if it had been planned.

Session 4: Croxteth Hall and Victorian and Edwardian Costume. We started with a chat about our visit, sitting on the carpet. Each child talked about his favourite part of the Hall and the one he disliked most. Most of them disliked the huntsman and the dead deer but one boy had no views on this saying that he 'liked it all', which saved him thinking and making any decision! This chat should really have come during the afternoon of our morning visit but administration prevented this, and the holiday the following Monday meant that we were talking about a visit one week after it took place. This was too far distant for correct memory and enthusiasm for this age-group.

The children then returned to their tables and worked on a 'Match up the pictures with the words' sheet. This involved recognising the picture models in the Hall, reading nine names (e.g. greyhound, moat, pheasant) and putting the two together. The first 'match' was done for the children. After about ten minutes we checked them and most children had complete success. This skill of matching picture (object) with word, helped by our visit, was a good exercise, which could well be developed for other topics.

Work was then started on Lord Sefton's main coach which, since it is kept in Merseyside Museum, we had not actually seen. I asked questions about where Lord and Lady Sefton sat, and who sat outside, how many horses would draw it, and who mended the wooden wheels. This last question linked our visit to the wheelwright's base at the Hall to Lord Sefton's coach. We talked about colours for the coach and the children completed a sentence at the bottom of the picture and coloured the coach blue and gold. We gained information about colours from a museum postcard.

We further developed our visit to Croxteth Hall by looking at coloured postcards and pictures from *Pictorial Education* made into displays of 'Fashion 1882-1920' and 'Children's Clothes', and leisure pursuits of the same dates. Booklets from Platt Hall Museum of Costume, Manchester, were very useful references in this respect, as well as a booklet from Croxteth Hall called *High Society 1875-1920*. The children were particularly intrigued by boys wearing sailor suits and playing with whips and tops. I promised to bring an antique dolls' tea set similar to one depicted on one of the postcards. Two of the postcards had additional historical interest as they were nineteenth-century paintings. Other unusual toys were a Noah's ark with animals, and a pedal horse, a wooden horse on wheels. The children then completed colouring outlines of boys' clothes in 1893 and 1907, men's suits in 1800 and 1914 (in both cases showing differences) and a lady's bustle dress of about 1870.

Session 5: Life at Croxteth Hall in 1900. The first part of this session was spent in arranging how my ten children would tell the rest of their class about our work. In five pairs it was decided that the following topics would be undertaken by the children:

1. The showing of twelve slides of Croxteth Hall
2. The Molyneux family

3. Our visit to Croxteth Hall
4. Children's clothes
5. Ladies' fashion

After that we talked about how 'upstairs' and 'downstairs' lived at Croxteth Hall, and using words on the blackboard, the children completed a short composition. Some of the group might have been able to write this themselves, as was shown by the composition they did with the class teacher on their visit to Croxteth Hall. On the other hand my 'summary' of life at the Hall was a difficult piece of work for children to arrange in sentences as it was not an 'account' of what *they* had done. Towards the end of this session we looked at a picture of one of the first motorcars of 1907, the sort used by the Molyneux family and seen at the north front of the Hall in one of the family photographs, with a chauffeur standing at the side.

Session 6: Telling the Rest of the Class about our Work on Croxteth Hall. In spite of much help from the class teacher, the preparation of the five 'lecturettes' proved more difficult than we had anticipated. Although the children remembered their material and had notes on postcards, they became embarassed if they made mistakes. They had to learn to look at the visual aids and talk from them. With help from the class teacher and my working of the slide-projector we managed, though the rest of the class became restive at times. I had brought two genuine nineteenth-century artefacts with me. One was a pure silk wedding dress of 1857 belonging to one of my ancestors, and the other was the dolls' tea service. I left these at the school until the class teacher completed all the work. About ten days later I returned to the school to look at the children's completed work. This had been extended to include poor people as well as rich, with large pictures made by my group of their own choice, such as the official robes of Lord and Lady Sefton, Lord Sefton's carriage and the 1572 Hall. The class as a whole had made nineteenth-century paper plates and the Queen Anne front of the Hall in a collage supported by examples of brass articles (to link on to the Sefton brasses).

Resources for the Topic of Croxteth Hall

Teachers of infants seldom choose an historical topic because of lack of resources provided by publishers and local authorities. Junior teachers can usually rely on a textbook, even of a chronological kind, and although this is inadequate, it is a beginning, and can be built on as the years go by. The topic we undertook was also more difficult in that it was local history, and not directly written about by any national publisher. The reason that our topic of Croxteth Hall was successful was on the whole that I collected materials over several weeks and the class teacher used them and her expertise to improve my basic information. Once these materials have been collected for a topic lasting half a term, they should be kept (including the children's work) and used another year. Thus for this, and many other Infant Schools in Liverpool and district, Croxteth Hall could be built into the scheme of work, and entirely new topics avoided each year. The materials should also be at the disposal of other teachers in the school, and should be kept (in several copies) in the LEA Humanities Resources Centre.

I will discuss the resources we used under five headings: buildings; books and other materials; artefacts; disposable materials such as coloured paper, glue etc; and artistic work done by the children themselves. A teacher must tap five different sources for information, involving visits and much work done out of school.

Buildings. The central feature of all our operations was Croxteth Hall itself, and work on a stately home is best not undertaken unless an appropriate and accessible building is available in the district and there are educational facilities there. I paid the Hall three visits before I took the children. Although all of the Hall available for inspection was not suitable for 6-year-olds, I was given a free hand and could go where I wanted. No young child could expect to understand the complicated architecture of a four-hundred-year-old house, but our purpose was not to do this, and selected parts of the building could be made into a whole for them. The atmosphere of the building also gave them much help in understanding the past.

Other sources of help were the staff at the Merseyside County Museum, and its excellent Education Service which provided workbooks which could be photocopied, with postcards and pamphlets. The Archives Department of the Central Library also houses early twentieth-century photographs of Croxteth Hall, which were copied for me. The Children's Library of the Central Library and two Branch libraries willingly lent selected books for the allotted time and made efforts to get other books, on old houses, costume, toys, heraldry, Liverpool's history and the Victorian and Edwardian periods.

The LEA Resources Centre allowed cheap facilities for photocopying the more complicated pictures which very young children would have found difficult to copy. The only trouble was that a car was essential to get to this centre, which could easily have hindered some teachers.

Books and Packs. A bibliography of books helpful locally and nationally will be given at the end of this unit. They fall into five categories: old houses, costumes, toys, Victorian and Edwardian social life, heraldry, and books on Liverpool. The local books will obviously be different for different areas of the country. I also found 'Dinosaur' books and 'Squirrel' outline pictures very useful for children. Many of the books are more useful for teachers, as few suitable History books are yet published for 5 to 7-year-olds.

I also used local packs. The teachers' pack for Croxteth Hall was essential, but one must be selective, as much of the material is more suitable for 7 to 11-year-olds and older pupils. Merseyside Museums publish a very useful folder *The Rich and Poor in 19th Century Liverpool* and Liverpool LEA has produced a folder *Town under Siege: Liverpool in the Civil War 1642-4*, in which an excellent picture of Liverpool Castle is produced and can be copied.

Artefacts. These are the staple diet of young children for learning about the past. Many artefacts were on show at Croxteth Hall but could not be handled by the children as they were in cases or railed off. The brass objects for their display in the vestibule at school were brought by the class teacher and children, but were not all as old as 1882 to 1920. My 1857 wedding dress and nineteenth-century children's tea service were genuine artefacts. They could be handled and talked about in the classroom. With more time, artefacts of 1882 and 1920 could have been developed as a topic to illustrate the social life of the period.

Disposable Materials. With the increasing expense of paper, card, glue, crayons etc., with cutbacks in education, large sheets of paper for display purposes are precious, and should be kept as far as possible for future use. The school let me have varying sizes of coloured paper on to which I fixed postcards, pictures from *Pictorial Education*, pictures from packs and from Merseyside Museum Service. I also used large pieces of white paper for the time-line. A4 sheets of duplicating paper were also consumed as each member of the group had several sheets for each session. There was also a need for a variety of coloured crayons, adequately sharpened, and also for several large display boards as well as a blackboard. I was fortunate that the school, with falling numbers, was able to provide a large room with a table/chair area, and a carpeted one, which was also supplied with a display board, screen, projector on a stand and blackboard. Thus during the hour-and-ten-minute session, I could vary the seating and physical activity of the children; they also had plenty of room to move about and look at the visual aids.

Work Done by the Children. This was a resource from which other children as well as themselves could learn, and their work, if preserved, could form a future resource for teaching purposes. Each child involved in my group built up the coloured workbook I made for them called 'Croxteth Hall'. This included completed A4 sheets of information worked on each session. They also contributed to a large book entitled 'Our Visit to Croxteth Hall' which was made up of accounts of their visit by each child. In addition, they worked in pairs on large pictures of their own choice, such as the official robes of Lord and Lady Sefton, the carriage of Lord Sefton, the Molyneux coat-of-arms, Liverpool Castle and the 1572 front of the Hall. The class as a whole started with discussions and pictures of houses generally as an introduction to stately homes. Terraced houses, semi-detached houses, detached houses, bungalows, flats and high-rise flats, such as those at Croxteth seen at the hall, were discussed. The class as a whole made a large collage of the Queen Anne front of the Hall for the school entrance hall and collected brass utensils to link up with the replicas of brass rubbings seen at the Hall. They also wrote about homes in Victorian times, including poor as well as rich, and made a big frieze of black-and-white Victorian working-class homes (Figure 6.5). Some children wrote about, and made pictures of, Victorian fashion, in keeping with the display of upper-class fashion at Croxteth Hall.

Assessment

No formal assessment was made of the work, as accurate assessment with 6-7 year olds is very problematical. The children obviously enjoyed the work and remembered a great deal of factual material, as well as dates, especially one boy who had a natural inclination for them. They were also highly-motivated and willing during our sessions, though their abilities were varied. Due to the expertise of the class teacher and my provision of resources, the rest of the class was able to work on parallel but less specific lines and this back-up when I was not in school was a tremendous help to my group. During my account of the Unit I made some preliminary assessments as to the children's learning and my teaching as the work progressed.

Figure 6.5: Victorian Working-class Homes

I underestimated the differences in ability of the group, as I found that about half of the ten children could form their own sentences well and had no need of compositions made up by me to be completed by them. Nor did the group need the help of vocabulary on the board. I made the mistake of providing too many outline drawings and not allowing them enough scope for their own work, especially writing, so the activity became automatic crayoning, which was too easy and not varied enough for many of them. Their freehand work with the class teacher showed that they were more capable than I had anticipated. There was a need for a build-up of vocabulary in their workbooks on a special page, and constant reference to this. Many words were specialised terms, such as 'coat-of-arms', 'brass' and 'title', and the names of the different forms of sporting activity. My lettering on the visual aids should have been larger and bolder as well as more carefully-written, in keeping with the school's procedure. The children found talking about the work to the rest of the class difficult, and this might have been overcome by more practice in my sessions. With limited time at my disposal I probably did too much talking myself, and too much setting of tasks to be accomplished, instead of listening to the children talk. I was pleased to find that the time-line and dates did not cause any more problems than anything else. Although the children lived so near the city centre, few knew where Castle Street and the Victoria Memorial were, or the relationship of the River Mersey to them.

Above all my spasmodic appearances, instead of my teaching the class all the time, made the work too limited in contrast to the actual Hall. It could have been developed to the home farm at Croxteth Hall, the Wildlife Gardens, the wheelwright's workbase, costume on a broader scale, and the Victorian poor of Liverpool. The class teacher did this to a large extent, incidentally as well as specifically, and could have done more with deeper knowledge and resources at her disposal.

The fact, however, that this experienced and able class teacher regretted that I had not taught the whole class and taken them all to Croxteth Hall is some sign of successful assessment.

References

For teachers:

G. Chandler, *Liverpool* (Batsford, 1957).
Croxteth Hall Country Park (Merseyside County Council, 1980).
M. Girouard, *Life in the English Country House* (Yale, 1978).
R, Innes-Smith, *An Outline of Heraldry* (Pilgrim Press, 1973).
J. Lofthouse, *Lancashire's Old Families* (Robert Hale, 1972).
C. Mackinnon, *The Observer's Book of Heraldry* (Warne Bros., 1966).
E. Midwinter, *Old Liverpool* (David and Charles, 1971). (The first Grand National, pp. 40-52).
N. Pevsner, *Buildings of England: South Lancashire* (Penguin, 1969).
The Rich and Poor in 19th Century Liverpool (Merseyside County Museums, 1979).
R.H. Wilmott, *Discovering Heraldry* (ULP, 1965).
D. Yarwood, *English Houses* (Batsford, 1966).

For teachers and children:

Clothes and Costume, Starters Long Ago (Macdonald, 1974).
Gallery of English Costume Picture Books (Manchester Corporation, 1949-63).
M.G. Graham-Cameron, *Life on a Country Estate* (Dinosaur, 1978).
H. Hansen, *Costume Cavalcade* (Eyre Methuen, 1956).
M. Harrison, *Growing Up in Victorian Days* (Wayland, 1980).
High Society, A display of formal dress for fashionable people, 1875-1920 (Merseyside County Council, 1980).

M.S. Macdonald-Taylor, *Furniture* (OUP, 1961).
A. Schofield, *Toys in History* (Wayland, 1978).
A. Scott, *One day in Victorian England* (Tyndall, 1974).
J. Shepherd, *Edwardian Times*, Picture Panorama of British History, (Mills and Boon, 1977).
M. Sichel, *Costume Reference, The Victorians* (Batsford, 1978).
M. Sichel, *Costume Reference, The Edwardians* (Batsford, 1978).
G. Wills, *Victoria: Later Years*, 1885-1900, The English Life Series (Wheaton, 1967).

Unit II: Integrated Unit on Caves with 5 to 7-year-olds

This unit used Caves as a stimulus for teaching Place and Time as well as other disciplines in the integrated day. As this type of work is less structured than others it will not be considered under quite the same headings; it was taught and written by Pat Raper.

The School and Children

I used this topic over a period of a term in a two-form entry village infant school which is separate from the junior school. The village is used by a cross-section of inhabitants, commuters to London and Oxford, as well as an old-established farming community. Fathers' occupations varied from the lower working class to managerial/professional groups. Most parents showed great interest in school activities and we achieved an outstanding record of visits, support and co-operation. The class was family-grouped in a limited team situation consisting of the age group 5 to 7+. All the children worked on individual programmes within an integrated day. As there were children with some learning and/or social difficulties, grouping was dictated only by chronological or learning needs. These were well integrated within friendship groups. The younger children spent more time on play, pre-reading and art activities.

Stimulus for the Topic

The topic was chosen as a result of some children's visit to some caves and stories read about them. The older children had shown great interest in volcanoes, a short project undertaken in the winter term. As the spring term usually limits outdoor activities, I wanted to base my umbrella project on a subject mainly from available library books, stones found in our environment and as a preparation for an environmental topic in the summer term. I aimed to give each child the experience of contributing on a personal level, as well as learning to co-operate within a small group. As the concept of caves developed in the widest sense, I hoped that the children would learn to enquire whenever possible into the reasons for their existence, where one might find them (i.e., structures and textures), the social aspects of caves in terms of a place to live, hide in and for shelter. I set no limits to the children's enquiries or the eventual scope of the project other than the desire to learn, observe and enquire. The project would have its roots in a continuous comparison of time and place with our present environment. As it could be undertaken in any infant school, perhaps it needs stressing that many aspects of the topic were woven into mathematical and reading situations.

Preparation with the Children

This started with a complete involvement of the whole class in a discussion of 'how we can find out'. I made a plan providing a basis for dividing the topic in such a way that small groups as well as individual children could explore their own interests, while still contributing to a comprehensive study. The children were divided into three activity groups of Stoneshapes, Explorers and Rescuers. The topic of caves has its roots in literature, archaeology, history, geology and geography, with the overall aim of participation and 'doing'.

My first step was to make a list of the actual words used by children of what they really understood by the word cave, and the question of who could make a home in one. The children helped with this. Here is the exact list, which is vital as a first assessment of my topic plan:

Cave: Tunnel; a dig; a jagged place; a stony place; a place where one could be frightened; a dirty place; seaside; something very dark; horrid; a cracked place; something made of stones; spooky; bumpy sides; I like it because you can cook there; wet; my daddy found something looking like gold; rocky; finding money perhaps; haunted; looking for animal tracks; poking fingers into holes; slipping; dragons and monsters; not me alone

Who can live there?: Tigers; rats; foxes; wolves; cave people of long ago; people in Jesus' time; bears; birds; bats; lizards; rabbits; insects; spiders; frogs; birds making nests; girls playing houses; worms; caterpillars; butterflies; ladybirds; snakes; dead animals found in stones — fossils; skeletons; fish if there was water; no crocodiles — they like it warm; a chicken that has run away and hides; giants; not me; not my friends; too cold to stay there.

The next step would be looking for and ordering books and film-strips. We were very fortunate to have an excellent relationship with the library service. Although the library van only visited our school once a term, books were sent whenever we wanted a selection. I cannot speak too highly of the helpful and patient ways of our librarians. Their suggestions were wide and imaginative, saving me endless time in preparation. All books would be in our classroom on constant display so that everybody could browse at leisure. In this way the children could follow their own interests and have their ideas challenged. As soon as the bookbox arrived the children were involved with sorting, thereby learning what is a reference, story or fiction book. Some of the reading books were slightly graded into large print illustrations and vocabulary; I do not believe, however, in ever restricting the use of any book. It is most interesting to watch this book activity and how aware the children were of presentation. I find this a vital aspect in the preparation of learning situations. Perhaps one also needs to stress the importance of watching that reference books are up-to-date.

The next step was to list and contact the 'human' resources, such as parents, teachers and local people who might have special knowledge or who would be willing to help. Parents have needed little persuasion to come and talk to either the class or a small group in a very informal way. We were also very fortunate to get pictures and photographs as a source of information. Learning to sort these, and discussing them, proved a very valuable activity. Needless to say, I value parental involvement, and can speak highly of their help.

If I were to sum up the preparations for such a topic I would list them as follows:

1. Making a list of all the aspects of the project, however haphazard to start with, including my own reading in philosophy, history and geography.
2. Discussing and talking to the children as often as possible to get a feeling of 'what is of interest' and to develop their oral skills.
3. Making an outline plan for the children so that every group or child knows what they wish to explore, with a record of responsibilities. Be prepared to change this when necessary, so learning *how* to learn.
4. Making a chart of questions which should or could be asked all the time, and displaying this in the work area to develop story-writing, vocabulary and other learning skills. These could include: What is it? How can we find it? When did it happen? How does it

feel if you touch or smell it? How did it happen? Does it talk-see-think-hear? Who is involved? Which book do you need? Who did it?

5. Having and collecting a wide selection of junk material, the right glue, stories, music, film-strips, books and other resources.
6. Preparation of learning materials which integrate basic learning and mathematical computation.
7. Collecting and organising a varied selection of books for the class-room as graded reading material in order to develop library skills.

The topic of caves can be of great interest on a variety of levels. For the younger child it is a great opportunity to explore textures and shapes, to see, to touch and to experience. We collected stones, made them out of clay, painted them, shaped ourselves as stones in PE and Drama and looked for stones and assembled them into caves. We made an enormous cave, which the children used as a play area, including an underwater area made by draping cellophane paper about a foot from the ground. Although I intended exploring a specific cave, I found that the children were more interested in exploring an imaginary cave in which animals existed and in making cave drawings that could tell us that somebody had lived there. I prepared a Drama story in which we physically explored such an imaginary cave, the necessary equipment used and techniques of survival.

How the Unit was Taught

As the work pervaded much of the integrated day it is impossible to think of it in 'sessions'. The following examples are some of many which we worked out and I call them 'movement stories':

Exploring a Cave. I asked each of the children to imagine they were in a cave as I said: 'I have a rope tied around me. My hand gropes in front, then to the left, then to the right, then above my head, then where my feet are. Everywhere I touch is rock. It is very dark and I close my eyes to feel better. Suddenly I can sense something strange and craggy and next to it a crack. I stop and listen. From far away I can hear a faint noise, first weak, then stronger, then hissing, then faint again; I wonder what it can be. I tie my rope round a jutting-out rock to make sure I shall find my way back. One hand touches the rope and with the other I stretch and explore. I take a slow step forward and another, but in the darkness I hit my head on another spike. I stop and plan my next move. Slowly I feel with my hand and follow the rock downwards. Ha!

There is a gap. I crouch as low as I can and slide through the gap. I paddle through the water, slowly releasing my rope all the time. I reach another open space leading into a round chamber. Suddenly I pull at my rope, and find that it gives way and coils around my arms and legs. Every movement I make seems to make another knot. I must have broken it. What can I do? Just as I am working out what to do, the rope tightens around my leg. I fall over and crash against the cave wall. A hand touches my back and finds my arm. I have been found by my friend. I let myself be dragged forward and then sideways, easing myself gently through the gap and the water. At last I hear my friend exclaim, "We're safe".'

From this we passed on to the early cave-dwellers, by suggesting that it was not only the mountains, ice or endless sand that made life hazardous and unpredictable but that nature too must have contributed, the rich plant life as much as the animals being aggressive and frightening. We then explored food sources, thought and compared what we could find in the way of berries, herbs, roots and shoots and bark, and discussed what a little cave child would like to find and eat. In my preparations I called this situation 'the victory over hostile surroundings'.

This led on to 'techniques of survival'. The need to cook food and conquer the cold, not to mention the fear of the dark and ways in which cave children would amuse themselves. It occurred to me that in spite of all our inventions today we have not adapted sufficiently to dominate our weather conditions. At this point the children's wide knowledge of television programmes and books showed itself. It would have been easy to leave the topic and explore ingenious ways human beings have tamed the elements through the ages. I felt though that these cave people, in spite of a life governed by daily struggles for survival had left us beautiful cave paintings and artwork that has been called an unwritten poetry. Having touched on some aspects of primitive life, we returned to looking at caves and the creatures who can live there. It was not difficult to arouse interest in the wonders of the subterranean world with its raging rivers, lakes, crystals, twisting passages and stone formations. I mentioned that it is thanks to the pioneering enthusiasts that many of today's caves can be visited at all.

We then repeated our first movement story of exploring a cave and in this way I could assess progress of interest, depth of thinking, and acquisition of relevant vocabulary, all of them very marked.

Naturally the children's own creative stories were a reflection of the aspects of caves in which they were specifically interested. It showed without a doubt that being an explorer was what most of them found exciting, rather than being a prehistoric person or a later cave-dweller. We therefore devoted some time to the importance not only of wearing the right clothes and having appropriate equipment, but being aware of what team spirit really means. The danger of going alone was discussed and we remembered that safety for oneself depends upon safety for others. By suggesting that the inside of caves can be drastically changed by sudden rainfalls, explosions or road-building, most children found opportunities to be leaders of expeditions, rescuers and so on. By closing our eyes, we pretended to be in darkness. This gave an idea of the sense of the passing of time underground, and considerations of the effect it would have on breathing, equipment and general morale. 'How long is long?' brought great amusement to all of us, while providing a chance to bring in mathematical and historical time concepts. To sum up this aspect of the work, I aimed to explain to the children that all explorations anywhere depend very much on training, team spirit, patience and resourcefulness, not necessarily in that order, and that this overall spirit has a place too in our daily lives.

Our next step was to think about the varieties of caves and where one might find them. We wondered who had visited a cave, whether it was a dead or dried-out one, or one which had resulted from a volcanic explosion. As most caves visited by the children were by the seaside, we explored the influence of water on stone formation, and the dripping of water as seen in caves. We thought about this as a growth pattern, used it in art as a pattern-maker, and experimented making sugar and salt crystals. There was much that I would have liked to explore, such as comparing different cave structures and their past origins, but time did not allow this. All I hope is that the children's enthusiasm has been sufficiently awakened for it to be possible to build on to their knowledge at a later date.

Shape and Area. Using a PE lesson, we incorporated mathematical concepts useful in a Cave topic. First we collected shapes, a mathematical activity. They were the following: open, closed, boundaries, flat face, near, next, edges, rigidity, inside, outside, curves, filling up a space, gap. We explored the ordering/comparison of dimensions and the relationships between them, and areas of regular and/or irregular shapes; we named 2D and 3D shapes in the environment. Then we applied shape-words to fit cave-stone language, thus: round-cylindrical; folded-up; curled around another rock; shrunk back into a wall; compressed and flat; screwed-up, coiled, corkscrew, spiral; hanging-dropping; jagged-pointed-crooked; bent-curved-straight; hard-twisted; sharp-angular; serrated-ragged-cracked; broken-fragile-collapsed; spread out-narrow; wavy; snapped-split-scattered; in a pile, heap, gathered together, stacked; fabric-texture; construction-structure-formation.

After this we started our PE lesson. I gave these instructions without a story: 'Find a place in the hall. Make yourself into a sharp, angular stone, hard and twisted, spread out and near' (using words on the list). 'Jump and collapse on the floor. Find a friend and pretend you are one rock, coiled around, cracked and broken. Finish by piling up into a heap [great fun] and collapsing.' (I use the word 'freeze' when I want the children to hold a position.)

Space. This can be taught through another movement story, using the children in the three groups of Stoneshapes, Explorers and Rescuers. I asked the Stoneshapes to make rock formations in the hall in groups of not more than four children. Each group marked round its formation with a piece of chalk, so that everyone could see its shape. Sam and Lara went to explore the rock formations (caves); Jonathan and Emma-Jo went later to form the rescue party, and Sarah acted as the rushing water. As rocks can change formation through earthquakes, water or fire, the children moved the formation to suit the story, leaving gaps that can be narrow or wide. As Sam and Lara approached each group they 'froze' to form the shape they wanted, already having discussed what this was to be.

After these preparations I started the story, speaking the words while the children acted their roles. Here is the story:

'Pick me up from my home in the morning', says Sam to Lara, 'and I will show you a real cave by the sea. It will be low tide if we are early enough, so be ready by 5 o'clock. That should give us plenty of time to get there. I will tell Jonathan and Emma-Jo where we are going, and the time we will surface again, just in case we need help. Have you got the list of things we need? Do make sure that you check this properly. Remember how dependent we are on our equipment and its functions. Don't pack unnecessary things, as everything gets heavier and bulkier when you are tired, and test your wet suit'. (Sam and Lara then went to their own homes to sleep.)

'It is morning now, a sunny day and very dry. As Sam wakes up he phones first of all for the weather forecast. When he is satisfied that there will be no dangerous storms or heavy rainfalls he quickly gets ready and collects Lara who is already waiting.' (The children then got ready to move along a pretend track to the cave.) 'The track leads them across a field, which is rather boggy, so often they need to take large steps. Then they cross a little bridge, then the path goes downhill and they need to go over and around many big boulders'. (This part can be extended if time allows, remembering the aim of the story is *in* the cave). 'At last they hear the sound of the battering waves and know they are near the cave. Before they enter, they stop, put on their helmets, test lights and torches, sit down for a minute and eat an apple each.

(Now is the time for the rocks to get into position. Leave some passages. Freeze your shapes. Relax when you are tired, and get into your 'shape' again when Sam and Lara are near you.)

Lara and Sam enter the cave. There is almost silence as they start off, and only a faint drip, drip is heard from somewhere in the depths of the darkness. It is black; no outlines can be seen, and they switch on their helmet lights and torches. They take very careful steps, and stop and listen intently, as the echo might tell them something of the rock and stones' fabric. It is very eerie in this black nothingness. I wonder if they are a little frightened. First they look straight ahead, all around the space, which is not lit up, which seems to be perpetual night, the darkness revealing only the outline of shapes. With their free hands they test the space near them and in front of them.

As they walk along they see a long narrow passage in front of them, with two very jagged and pointed rocks jutting out, often leaving only very narrow gaps to squeeze through. "Watch out", says Sam suddenly, "there's a hole. It may be slippery", but as he shines his torch he sees it is quite clean and dry. The passage seems to stretch endlessly between rocks that are coiled around one another and reach up high, higher than six double-decker buses piled up on one another. The grey walls soar up magnificently, and as Lara shines her torch she sees stalactites and stalagmites, which are beautiful to look at. But looking up is hazardous, as she nearly walks into a gigantic boulder. Watch out — it has broken into fragile little pieces. They must have fallen off a column. As they clamber over stones and rocks, they find that the passage narrows and they have to get down on to their knees, and, at one point, slide on their stomachs, quite a difficult thing to do with all their equipment on their backs. Just as they want to stand up, they hear another snap and more small fragments of limestone fall and just miss them. How grateful they are for their protective helmets. They shudder slightly, quite afraid of what might have happened if the stones had fallen on them.

But often when something nasty happens, something good happens straight afterwards. Their helmet lights illuminate a new area in the cave. They gasp, as they have never seen anything like this. Stalactites, stalagmites, helicites, curtains, straws, gourpools and cave pearls all sparkle with fairytale beauty. All these were formed by limestone rocks, dissolved and built up again with muted colours taken from the mineral deposits above. Water dripped gently, with a special rhythm, drip, drip, drip, drip, always the same.

Sam suggests a rest and he and Lara sit down to munch a sandwich and a piece of chocolate. Suddenly, without warning, there is a terrific noise. Both recognize the thing cavers fear most — rushing water. Lara and Sam quickly pick up all their equipment and look out for the highest safest boulder they can find near them. They climb up onto it. "This will do", says Sam. "We can be safe here for a while. It must be a thunderstorm, but it will only be short. I checked with the weather station and nothing was forecast. Let's put on our wetsuits though, just to be safe." Lara wonders how they will find their way back with all the water gushing through the narrow passages through which they have just come. But there is no time to think. Quickly they put on their wetsuits and climb a little higher. Terrifying as the water is as it rushes around, it is a beautiful sight to see how the rocks start to glisten and shine in the dark. Water reaches the rocks, cracking off a bit here, breaking off a bit there. Large heaps collapse into new piles of stone shapes, making passages where there had been none. The water foams around corners pounding against razor-sharp edges. Sam grips hard to his rock, warning Lara to do the same.'

(This is a good place to play a piece of music. My choice was Falla's *Ritual Firedance* and the theme from *The Legend of the Glass Mountain*. If children are restless, this is a good point to postpone the finish of the story to a later date or to story-time, just to listen to.)

'. . . So they sit and wait and watch how a peaceful cave can change into a dangerous one, where boulders roll around as if a giant is moving them, where pieces of rock fall from the roof and where the cold and wet can lead to injuries and hurt.

In the meantime Jonathan and Emma-Jo see the rainstorm, and knowing the danger of such a downpour they quickly get ready for the rescue, remembering to notify other club members of what they are going to do. Safety rules are important. They set out on the same track as Sam and Lara.'

Now finish the story, allowing for the children's interest and time available, thinking in terms of happy reunions, being safe again and what a lovely thing it is to have friends.

A follow-up to such a story could be:

Basic: giving every child a piece of paper with the instructions 'Please draw the shape of your rock or any rock'. (Teacher) writes with thick felt pen the words the child used. These papers are collected and put together and used as a basic reader in the book corner.

Or: giving each child a piece of paper with the instructions 'Please draw the part of the story you liked best of all'. (Teacher) writes with thick felt pen the words the child used to interpret the situation, then as above.

Or: giving each child a piece of paper, asking them to write and draw part or the whole story, or make up another one.

Or: dictating relevant vocabulary, with the children finding their own words, i.e., making word lists.

The Children's Own Work

This included work from workcards and workbooks for the younger or less able children. One aspect of work was the follow-up of drama stories by the children drawing a quick picture of what interested them most. They would then bring me their picture and I would write their own words as a heading with a thick felt pen. We would then bind all these pictures into a folder and this would be used as a reading book in our book corner. This was always a great favourite, as everybody had contributed. It also gave me a chance to talk to each child and assess the value of the lesson. The older children would usually follow this up with some creative writing.

Another aspect of 'cave' work was my dictation lessons for all abilities. The aim was to use the contribution of each child's words as the basis for dictation, involving writing and spelling skills. Each child had a Dictation Book of what I dictated, which he illustrated in bold crayons. Thus the story of 'Exploring a Cave' was illustrated by the children after the experience of the 'movement story' already given. The more able children would use dictionaries to find some of their own words for their own stories while the younger and less able came to me to ask how a specific word was written, thus combining language skills and topic skills. These dictation lessons took place at least three times a week early in the morning when the children were fresh.

Resources

We collected an enormous number of cardboard boxes which we piled up as the basic mountain shape, leaving a large entrance for the 'play cave'. We left the open side of the box facing outside so that children could work on their own individual caves. The boxes were then covered with newspapier mâché, disguising the straight sides with crumpled paper to give a more realistic shape to the mountain. When this structure was dried hard we textured the surface using polyfilla and stones, dried seedhead and twigs collected by the children from their own gardens, as well as during walks around the school. A mixture of porridge and paint hardens well to give the impression of a craggy surface and this is an opportunity for achieving different colour surfaces. We painted with liquid clay, inks, and soil mixed with paint and water, standing on chairs and tables to reach the top of the mountain, and getting really messy, with an end result that was much admired by everybody.

We made animals and people out of clay, papier mâché and pipe-cleaners, and this livened up each cave. Time was well-reflected in this as the children made their own 'fossil' imprints, hiding people, monsters and so on. All this was a good base for creative writing and language development.

Each child had a drawing book for drawings on a small scale while large pictures were displayed all around the classroom, wherever possible. My aim throughout this term's work was that the presentation of the topic should be appreciated by the whole class, so that its influence was vital to the progress of learning. It is a great opportunity to help one another take pride in one's environment.

Assessment

There was no formal evaluation of this topic work other than that it gave the children great enjoyment, which was constantly visible. It gave me a chance, in an indirect way, to give confidence and help to those children who had specific emotional and learning needs. Many opportunities existed to arouse and satisfy curiosity as well as develop thoughts from pure guesswork to imaginative interpretation in the widest sense. I found that my own knowledge was often challenged by the children's very penetrating questions, which gave all of us a chance to learn from 'not knowing' and finding out together. This process of 'not knowing' and realising that one cannot know everything, gave great confidence in the learning situation so that making mistakes was seen as important a step as finding out. Participation meant art and craft, discussions, and movement stories as well as the childrens' own creative written work. They all reflected the real interest everybody had in the subject. The whole class showed a tremendous sense of fair play, which meant the 'spirit' of weakness, strength and other human attributes could be interpreted within the classroom environment for the benefit of all.

Many of the older children wanted to pursue their own lines of thought the following term. Eight children became especially interested and wanted to know more about cave-dwellers and pre-historic times. Six boys wanted to explore fossils and learn more about extinct animals. The majority of younger children wanted to have a holiday-adventure story. Many parents followed up by taking their own children to specific caves and museums.

References

For Teachers

E. Bauer, *The Mysterious World of Caves* (Collins, 1971).
B.L. Bedford, *Challenge Underground* (Allen and Unwin, 1975).
J. Bradford, *Man is an Artist* (Harrap, 1957).
W.C. Cartner, *Fun with Geology* (Kay and Ward, 1971).
What is the Earth? Pageant of Knowledge Series (Collins, 1965).
C. and J. Crosby, *Physical Geography in Colour* (Ward Lock, 1969).
M.L. Davies, *The Coast* (Muller, 1977).
R. Edwards and R. Guerin, *Aboriginal Bark Paintings* (Hale, 1973).
M. Edel, *The Story of People* (Bodley Head, 1959).
M. Farr, *The Darkness Beckons: a History and Development of Cave Diving* (Diadem Books, 1980).
P. Francis, *Volcanoes* (Penguin, 1976).
V. Mazak, *Prehistoric Man* (Hamlyn, 1980).
R. Richards, *Holes, Gaps and Cavities* Schools Council Science 5-13 (Macdonald, 1973).
F. Quilici, *Primitive Societies* (Collins, 1972).
D. Roe, *Prehistory* (Paladin, 1970).
P. Sauvain, *Prehistoric Britain* Imagining the Past (Macmillan, 1979).
N. Thomas, *Guide to Prehistoric England* (Batsford, 1960).
S. Thompson, *Early Man* Fact Finders (Macmillan).
R.F. Willets, *Everyday Life in Ancient Crete: Cave and cave cults, scripts and records* (Batsford, 1970).

For Children

P. Biegel, *The King of the Copper Mountains* (Collins, 1973).
— *The Seven Times Search* (Dent, 1971).
— *The Dwarfs of Nosegay* (Blackie, 1978).
E. Colwell, *Tales from the Islands* (Kestrel, 1975).

E. Hamilton, *The First Book of Caves* (Ward, 1956).
Ladybird Readers: *Mountains, Water, Dinosaurs, Homes, Underground, The Tree and its World, The Stream, Forests*.
Macdonald Starters: *Caves, Rain, Fire, Colours, Dinosaurs, Homes, Buried History, Stone Age Man, Cooks and Kitchens*.
Macdonald Junior Reference Library: *The Earth, Rocks and Minerals*.
Macdonald Visual Books: Easy Reading Edition.
R. Manning, *Green Smoke* (Kestrel (Penguin), 1975, 1967).
— *Dragon in Danger* (Longman (Penguin), 1972, 1971).
— *Dragon's Quest* (Kestrel, 1973).

Audio-visual Material:

M. Neurath, *Cavemen and Hunters* (Longman/Common Ground).
Colour filmstrip with notes.

Unit III: Time Unit on the Peasants' Revolt (1381) with 8 and 9-year-olds

I taught this unit of work on this famous historical event over a period of three weeks' 'intensive' teaching, involving two lessons a week.

The School and Children

The school chosen for this experiment was a JMI School in the Toxteth area of Liverpool. In contrast to the Unit I school, this was in an unstable working-class area into and from which families were constantly moving; it was racially mixed and many buildings were derelict. There had been serious street riots here during the previous summer (1981). The numbers in the school were declining, and my class of sixteen children had decreased from the previous year's twenty-four, although four new children had been admitted from other local schools. So my small group was very insecure, showing this by incessant fidgeting with things on their desks, with the consequent loss of essential pencils and crayons, and much opening of desk lids and the conduct of personal quarrels with each other in class. In addition, there had been lack of firm class-control during the year. As in most single-stream schools the spread of ability was very wide, ranging from non-readers to a reading age of fourteen years.

The school building dated from the early part of the century. It was large and rambling, with several entrances into the playground. Our classroom was partitioned from the next one, had double desks, plenty of space (though little display space) and a clothes' stand at the back for coats. This single-stream school had a mixed sex staff which was very friendly, competent and philosophical. My group of children proved so difficult initially for me to control that I had to divide the class into two groups of eight, according to ability, and to concentrate my methods on those which would ensure some attention was given and work was done. As the topic chosen was of a narrative nature it could not be understood unless certain sequential events were learnt and places found on maps. This amounted to class teaching of a didactic kind, with plenty of individual activity and little movement about the classroom. I had tremendous support from the headmaster and deputy headmaster, and we all believed at the end, as did the children, that something had been learnt and enjoyed.

Preparation of the Unit

Since the Peasants' Revolt was a much-used national topic in 1981, preparation should have been easier than for Unit I. Yet most of the help given by publications was for children aged 9 to 13 or more, and had to be adapted. I also found that a detailed knowledge of London and places in the south-east of England was needed. The need for an understanding of Place was never more apparent in Time study than in this unit.

My first form of help came from the ILEA Centre for History and Social Sciences at Clapham, London, which I was able to visit.[1] The History Advisory teacher for secondary History had just prepared a folder of pictures (contemporary and otherwise), documentary material, and his own narrative on the Peasants' Revolt. He willingly allowed me to use his work, very relevant to London school children. This material used many of the more detailed studies, such as Mary Price's *The Peasants' Revolt* ('Then and There' series, Longman, 1980), but simplified them; I simplified them further.

Other forms of preparation were reading and note-making from reading books suitable for junior secondary children (see Bibliography), and *Essex and the Peasants' Revolt* (Essex Record Office, 1981) which contains a detailed 'Sequence of Events' sheet, day by day, from 6 December 1380 to 14 December 1381. In addition I sent for large visual aids from Pictorial Charts Ltd.[2] and the Tower of London. Then I began to make my own large visual aids, mostly diagrammatic maps and A4 worksheets of pictures and activities for the children. The school gave me plenty of large sheets of white and coloured paper as a basis for the large visual aids and for making a variety of coloured workbooks for the children's individual work. It duplicated the worksheets for me and collected library books from the Central Reference Children's Library. I also borrowed books from two Branch libraries. I had many of the illustrations from the Clapham Centre photocopied at Liverpool Resources Centre, having previously gained copyright permission from publishers and other concerned bodies. This facility can only be used if preparation is made well in advance. A school is well-advised, therefore, to repeat topics and 'refuel' with materials (until each primary school owns a photocopier — to me more important than a computer!).

The preparation thus involved reading, note-making, visits, lesson preparation, making children's books and visual aids, as well as writing to publishers. Any study as detailed as this, requires accumulation of considerable information. One of the children remarked that the text-book (a chronological four-book series) had only three sentences at the bottom of the page on the Peasants' Revolt, whereas we had spent three weeks on the topic! How did I find out about all this new material? Was the textbook wrong to leave it out?

Content

Although this unit was concerned with an event lasting only six months (compared with the one hundred years of Unit I) its intensity linking the violent events and reactions of peasants, King Richard II and his advisers, was in some ways more easily comprehended than a longer period. Unit I was concerned with social history, the way of life of a local aristrocratic family, interrupted by two World Wars. This unit was concerned with political as well as social and economic history and was nationally orientated, with London as its hub (though there were minor risings in the Midlands and other parts of the country). The factual nature of the work and the interplay of characters under strain was particularly appropriate to these children, who were able to empathise with both 'sides' in the struggle, and in some cases to compare their own reactions to the events in Toxteth in 1981 with the events in London in 1381. The fact that the drama was played out mainly in London and that a plan of London was used, in no way dismayed the children, many of whom had paid visits to the capital and knew about the Tower of London, the River Thames, St Paul's Cathedral and Westminster Abbey, as well as Canterbury Cathedral. So the language and concepts proved not too difficult for 8-year-olds. Many of my class came from large families and were well able to sympathise with the problem faced by Richard II, placed in between the 'two fires' of rebels and his own advisers, with all their personal jealousies. I was surprised how well these city-dwelling children understood the mainly agricultural nature of English society in the fourteenth century. They could also read contemporary illustrations from medieval manuscripts with ease.

During the six sessions the work came to be studied under seven headings:

1. The medieval peasant and his hard life
2. The Black Death of 1348
3. The beginning of the revolt in Essex and Kent, May-June 1381
4. London in 1381
5. Blackheath and Rotherhithe, 12-13 June 1381
6. The rebels enter London, 13-14 June 1381
7. Meeting at Smithfield, 15 June 1381

These seven topics could well have taken more than the six hours at my disposal. I would advise a permanent teacher to take at least one after-noon each week for seven weeks for them. I shall write my account imagining that I took this time.

How the Unit was Taught

Each of the six sessions lasted one hour, and in view of this particular class it was an advantage to have the sessions on two consecutive days. After the sessions, as in Unit I, I stayed in the staff room and fastened children's work into their workbooks, marked short tests necessary to check on the previous lesson, and was at hand for any queries arising from the work from the children or the class teacher. During the sessions the children worked at double desks as far as possible, one child to each double desk, well spaced out to avoid controversies between the children. I had two large blackboards on which to put visual aids and new words. I always put out their workbooks and mate-rials for each particular lesson on their desks before they came in from the playground. Towards the end of my time, children would be waiting for me in the playground to unlock the classroom door, and to help me put out materials and pencils and put up visual aids and boardwork. I enjoyed this time as they chatted to me about their work and were particularly courteous and co-operative.

Session 1: The Medieval Peasant and his Hard Life. For this I depended a great deal upon the pictorial chart, 'The Medieval Peasant', which depicts a village with the four seasons of work centring around it. From one of these seasons I took the sketch of the Lord's Mill, drew it and had it duplicated for each child. This seemed to me to represent the strained relationship between the lord's bailiff (with his whip) and the peasant being forced to have his corn ground in the lord's mill, for which he paid. I had also prepared a time-line, The Peasants' Revolt 1381, putting the event in its time context and relating the 'medieval peasant' to it (Figure 6.6).

Figure 6.6: The Peasants' Revolt, 1381: Time-line

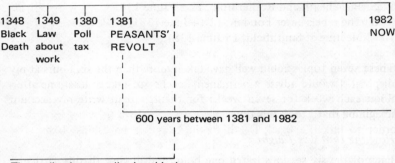

The medieval peasant lived at this time

We started the lesson with a discussion of the meaning of the words 'peasant' and 'revolt'. We decided that a peasant was a worker on the land, be it man, woman or child. The word 'revolt' meant the physical uprising of those with a grievance against those above them (compare 'riot'). This led to the meaning of a 'lord' and his relationship to King Richard and the peasants, and here some explanation of the feudal system was needed. We then looked at the picture of King Richard in the textbook and ascertained from his crown and throne that he was a king, although only fourteen years old.

From this introduction we looked at the time-line (both on the board and on the children's desks) and by counting back (in unison) found that the revolt happened about six hundred years ago. We also saw that the medieval peasant lived both before and after the revolt.

We then looked at the large coloured chart of The Medieval Peasant. In their textbooks there were pictures of how peasants lived and we tried to find out why this way of life made them unhappy. We came to the conclusion that they were very tired with overwork, in providing food both for the lord and for their own families. They were also unhappy because they had to pay money to the lord ('dues') for using his mill and other facilities (all written down in the Manor Record), as well as to the king for his 'poll tax' of 1380, on each person in a family above the age of fifteen. The peasant was also unhappy because his lord would not allow him to leave the village to find other work with another lord (i.e., he had no 'bargaining power' — compare trade unionists today).

The last part of this session was spent colouring the Lord's Mill picture in colours discussed as appropriate, yellow for the sack of corn and brown for the windmill's roof. There was discussion about how the corn was ground, by the 'sails' of the mill going round with the wind, and also of the fact that the mill could be swivelled round on its base to catch the right wind direction at whatever time of day it was needed. The link between corn, flour and bread was made, and the making of bread today from flour and yeast was discussed in view of the fact that most children ate shop-bought bread.

Session 2: The Black Death of 1348. This session started with a quick ten-point factual test on paper on the facts of the previous session in order to link the Black Death to the peasants' hardships. I gave the answers with help from the class, each child marked his own and handed the test paper in. From this recapitulation we looked back at the time-line for the date 1348 and found that it was over thirty years before 1381. Several children knew what form the plague took and described it in accurate detail. With the decrease in population owing to the Black Death lords had to consider their peasants more (law of 'supply and demand') and even pay them wages. The peasant could also now offer his services to another lord. King Richard soon stopped this by his 'Law about work', 1349 (Statute of Labourers) which forbade the peasant to leave his original village and put his wages back to what they had been, if he had received any at all, before 1348.

The second half of the session was spent in completing a four-point composition. The underlined first letters and gaps had to be supplied in the correct places from words on the blackboard. This type of work was helped by the short test at the beginning of the session. It was also an introduction to the reasoned and structured written work required of children writing about the past.

Session 3: The Beginning of the Revolt in Essex and Kent, May-June 1381. The central teaching aid for this work was a diagrammatic map of the River Thames, Essex and Kent and an outline of the coast. Again there was a large visual aid and each child had his own map. The map had four letters on it for important places, F (for Fobbing),

R (for Rochester), M (for Maidstone) and C (for Canterbury). A worksheet of six tasks helped the children to complete the map.

Most teachers could start from a large wall map of England and Wales (or individual atlases) and get children to find their own particular town in relation to London (in our case Liverpool). It is as well if Place work has familiarised 8-year-olds with a map of England and Wales. From this point we concentrated on London, Kent and Essex and compared the wall map with the enlarged diagram-map I had made.

Using this I told the story of how the king's tax-collector (of poll-tax) was attacked by the peasants of Fobbing in Essex. These peasant forces divided up, some marching into Kent to gain support, others going to London to see King Richard, and ransacking the houses of the wealthy as they went. The Essex peasants crossed the Thames and took Rochester Castle from its lord. They joined the Kent peasants at Maidstone, freed the rebellious priest, John Ball, from prison and made Wat Tyler their leader. Then they all went to Canterbury and burnt down the Archbishop's palace. The important position held by the clergy in advising the king in medieval times may be contrasted in discussion with Archbishop Runcie's role today. Is Archbishop Runcie in the Cabinet as was Archbishop Simon? The peasants burnt all the manor records, listing all the dues to be paid to the Archbishop as a lord. John Ball and Wat Tyler then urged the worn-out peasants, who had already walked a considerable distance, two hundred further miles to London to see King Richard. This feat may be compared with Marathon walks in 1983, completed as it was in two days. The narration of this story was done by question and answer, discussion and sensible use of the map.

Session 4: London in 1381. With the help of a plan in David Birt's booklet[3] I constructed a much simplified diagram of London in Chaucer's day, showing the River Thames, London Bridge, roads to Mile End and Blackheath, the city wall, the Tower of London, the Temple, St Paul's Cathedral, Westminster Abbey and Palace, the Wardrobe and the area known as Smithfield (Figure 6.7). I left spaces after letters in the map for the children to complete the labels. They could also crayon the river blue and the Tower and walls black.

Adapting the description of London by Jane Sayers[4] I read it to the class, asking them to find the places on their maps, already having the appropriate names on the blackboard. This is the account of London in 1381:

Figure 6.7: London and the Peasants' Revolt, June-July, 1381

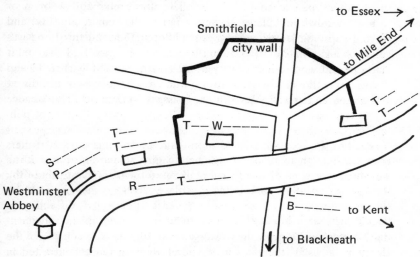

London was a very exciting city to live in. It had shops, streets, churches, chapels, gardens, a great bridge (London Bridge) and warehouses and docks. There were about 35,000 people living there. [There were only 1,000 people in Liverpool at the same time.] It was the biggest city in England and one of the biggest in the world. But it was very crowded because the city was only one mile square within the walls [the size of Sefton Park, Liverpool.] Cities in medieval times had walls to help to defend them against attackers.

Ships came into the port of London bringing goods from across the world — silks, wine and gold. They sailed up the River Thames as far as London Bridge. London Bridge had shops, houses and a chapel built on it and was one of the wonders of the world.

The king and his court were often in London. They stayed at the White Tower in the Tower of London, which belonged to the king.

There were gates in the city of London so that people could come in and go out. They were closed and barred at night to keep enemies out.

There were lots of inns, or pubs, in the London of 1381 for people to amuse themselves in and many shops, but these looked just like ordinary houses. They had no windows for showing or displaying things for sale, because glass was very expensive. Inside the shops people could buy woollen cloth, silks and wooden or pottery bowls and plates. If they were rich they could buy silver and gold cups and jewels and things made of leather and fur. Food was not bought in shops, but in the market. People lived over their shops and workrooms, or very near to the docks and market. Towering over the city was St Paul's Church. There was a Bishop of London and this was his church. Peasants worked on fields outside the city walls.

Reading an account seemed more calming for this particular class than teaching them orally. A teacher reading something from a book was more like work than a teacher talking to them! The last part of the session was spent in completing the place labels on their maps, using the larger version on display. As in the case of Session 3, the ability to handle plans as if looking down on them from an aeroplane was essential. A composition, with word gaps to fill in, was completed on 'London in 1381'. Those teachers who want to deviate here to the Tower of London could do so with the help of much useful information from it.[5] The importance of the Tower in national history cannot be exaggerated and resources on this topic will always be useful in the primary school.

Session 5: Blackheath and Rotherhithe, 12-13 June 1381. From this time forward, events centred round London and the diagram used in the last session was essential. The method of teaching was oral; narrative work using children's responses and the diagram of London, 'reading' contemporary illustrations, and listening to and discussing short contemporary and other extracts.

The rebels, led by Wat Tyler and John Ball, were marched rapidly from Canterbury to London, stopping at Blackheath (arrow marked direction on the diagram), where John Ball preached a famous sermon. Each child had a contemporary picture of John Ball[6] on a white horse (name marked on him), gesticulating during his stirring sermon, and encouraging his followers to proceed into London according to God's will, to put right the wrongs of oppression. Leading questions were asked about the picture[7] and a stirring extract read from Mary Price's book: 'Take good courage and make away with them all, kill the great lords of the kingdom, slay all judges, lawyers, root out every man who is harmful to the common good, for when the great ones have been cut off, all men will be free.'[8] The wisdom of these words was discussed and whether the peasants were being used by their leaders. The children were asked to write three sentences about this picture in a space at the foot of the picture.

A second contemporary picture was then 'read'. This was of Richard II coming in his barge down the River Thames from the Tower, accompanied by his advisers, to speak to the rebels. Authorities speak of this visit to either Rotherhithe or Greenwich. The picture was analysed by asking which figure was Richard, the names of the buildings in the background, the peasants (amazingly well-armed!) and the open fields. These fields were looked at again on the diagram of London which enabled the children to see the same area in a different representation. Then I read a stirring extract from Mary Price's book and got the children to try to understand both the point of view of Richard and the rebels. The peasants wanted Richard to land from his barge to talk to them, but they were shouting so noisily that Richard decided to return to the Tower. Why had he left Westminster Palace to live in the Tower? How would the peasants feel? This made them determined to cross London Bridge and get into London. They thought that Richard would not co-operate and so they became more violent.

At this point I used the ILEA pamphlet which has an excellent page called 'Decision: what should the king do?', outlining Richard's difficult position between peasants and lords and asking for discussion of his possible courses of action. We took each choice in turn and decided why it would be a good one or not, finally deciding that he should play for time (what a lesson for life: 'wait and see'), listen to the demands of the peasants and see what could be done later. I also used a coloured contemporary postcard of Richard II[9] fastened on to card, again asking leading questions through the picture:

1. This portrait was painted just before Richard's death. He was King of England from 1377 to 1399 (look at the time-line). He was fourteen in 1381. How old was he when he was murdered in 1399?
2. What precious jewels are in his crown and collar?
3. What material is his coat made of?
4. What language is 'Ricardus'? Why is it not in English?
5. Why does he look unpleasant? Look particularly at his eyes and mouth.

This made us wonder whether this man in the portrait (by an unknown artist) was playing for time because he was cunningly seeking absolute power over both lords and peasants. Was this perhaps why he was eventually murdered?

Session 6: The Rebels Enter London, 13-14 June 1981. The townsmen of London opened the gates of London Bridge to the rebels from Essex and Kent on 13 June and burning of important buildings began. Finding the places on the diagram of London, we traced the rebels' steps to the Savoy Palace, the home of John of Gaunt, the King's uncle. They burnt it down. They also attacked the Temple where their enemies, the lawyers, were trained. Richard then agreed to the peasants' requests for freedom from some labour services and heavy taxes as well as not being punished for rebelling.

Wat Tyler suspected that Richard had agreed to the meeting at Mile End in order to draw the rebels from the Tower of London where Archbishop Simon of Canterbury and other lords were hiding. We looked at the large photograph of the Tower from outside and used the sketch of the Tower (Figure 6.8) to show how the rebels entered and found their prey. While Richard and most of the peasants were at Mile End the remaining rebels overcame a small guard and murdered Archbishop Simon and his friends. We used another contemporary picture[10] showing the murder of the Archbishop, Sir Robert Hales, the lord in charge of the country's money, as the Chancellor of the Exchequer is now, and a monk called Brother Appleton. Which people the figures depicted could be guessed from the clothes they were wearing;

Figure 6.8: The Tower of London

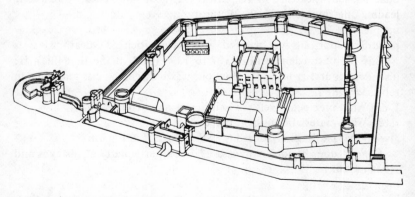

Source: *The Tower of London; its Buildings and Institutions,* John Charlton (ed.) (HMSO 1978).

we decided that the Archbishop had a tonsured head, the monk a cowl and Sir Robert Hales the clothes of a lord. Their severed heads were mounted on poles and stuck on London Bridge as an example to other lords. The rebels also murdered other people who came into their path.

When Richard returned from Mile End, he and his mother left the Tower and lived in 'The Wardrobe'. Wat Tyler had insisted on Richard writing down their agreement at Mile End. Richard had agreed to meet him and the rebels (some of whom had gone home by now, at Smithfield. What was Richard intending to do now that two of his chief advisers had been murdered? His behaviour at Smithfield would be crucial to the whole country, and his cunning had to better that of Wat Tyler.

Session 7: Meeting at Smithfield, 15 June 1381. This final crisis of the drama took place in a large open space at Smithfield, outside the city walls. We looked at our diagrams for this name. We used our final contemporary picture as well as the diagram of London. This picture is a double one, showing on the left Richard watching Mayor Walworth, Mayor of London, striking Wat Tyler, and on the right Richard offering himself as leader of the peasants after Tyler's death.[11] Wat Tyler was so confident that he rode away from the two thousand peasants towards the king, the Mayor of London and the accompanying lords. He quarrelled with Mayor Walworth whom he stabbed. But the Mayor was wearing armour under his clothes and he stabbed Tyler in return, and then the other lords also helped to murder him. Wat Tyler fell off his horse and died trying to return to the peasants. King Richard at once rode over to the rebels, pardoned them and offered to be their leader. The double story in one picture is interesting in showing that people who could not read learnt about past events through a story picture.

But Richard really had no intention of leading the peasants against his advisers and he broke his promises at Mile End and killed many rebels, including John Ball, the priest, in the south-east of England. I did not have time in six sessions to go into detail about how the rebels were crushed in St Albans and the south-east but Mary Price gives details in her book.[12]

I spent some time during the final session comparing the Toxteth Riots of 1981 and the Peasants' Revolt of 1381. More work could have been done on this as the children were very sensible, tried to understand all points of view, and discussed well. I divided the blackboard by a line, with 1381 on one side and 1981 on the other. On to this I wrote points of comparison as they arose in our discussions. Due to the great distance of time between these dates, six hundred years on the time-line, all facets could not be compared. For example more buildings were *burnt* in London than Toxteth because many more buildings were made of wood in the fourteenth century. Place was different as 1381 spread over a much larger area, the rebels had leaders and personalities were involved. In the end, in 1981 police and taxi men seemed to be immediate targets — officials mainly coming from 1981 'peasant stock', while in 1381 Richard's advisers were the targets. The position of Richard could not be convincingly compared with Mrs Thatcher's since he was a king and she was a people's representative, voted to power constitutionally. What they had in common was seeming oppression of poor by rich. As many young children were in the streets during the 1981 riots in Toxteth, it was most interesting to hear the reactions of these 9-year-olds. Were their views taken from older members of their families? Are 'the peasants' still revolting against oppression and economic crises? Political education would have to enter here.

Resources for the Unit on the Peasants' Revolt

The resources I used for this unit of work were more limited than for Unit I, partly because the particular class situation demanded fewer changes of method of work and partly because a local topic away from the particular locality (London) does not allow local visits, local arte-facts or the help of a museum. London schools can visit the Tower of London and the Museum of London, both well supplied for educational visits. My resources were books, packs, illustrative material, contemporary pictures and disposable materials, such as coloured sugar paper and card, various colours of magic marker and white drawing paper. The children did not put up a display, nor did we work with any other class, so the material signs of our work afterwards were individual workbooks. I have no doubt that if I were to work again with this class we should produce a greater variety of work.

Books and Packs. In the case of a national topic happening long ago I had to be the main source of information, especially as our only text-book covered the seven sessions in three sentences! The topic was also too specialised for this small school to have collected any appropriate illustrative material. I have given a Bibliography of suitable books for teachers and·children at the end of this unit. The most useful was Mary Price's *The Peasants' Revolt* (Longman, 1980) which is full of detailed narrative, contemporary accounts and illustrations. It also has an index, glossary, and 'things to do' section, with a 'How do we know?' section. Although too advanced for most 8 to 9-year-olds to read, it is ideal for the teacher's own preparation, and many extracts can be read or duplicated for the children to use and discuss. The other most useful book was David Birt's *Peasants' Revolt,* a Longman's Resource Unit (1974) presented in structured form, and again full of contemporary illustrations and extracts. It is intended as a workbook for junior secondary age children but can easily be adapted for younger juniors. It includes very helpful advice about activities for a class. London schools have the great advantage of the support of the History and Social Sciences Teachers' Centre from whom I gained much help through the photocopied pack on the Peasants' Revolt. This was compiled to provide activity and promote thought and discussion. Some of the children borrowed my copy of Crowther and Schofield's book of Action History cartoons of the story of the Peasants' Revolt (Arnold, 1977). It has activities after the cartoons such as a crossword, a role-playing exercise and a composition to complete with appropriate words. The Essex Record Office publication also has detailed documentation on the Essex rebels.

Illustrations. Finding information through looking at pictures was an effective method of teaching for a class of such wide abilities. Large visual aids suitable for class teaching were the chart of The Medieval Peasant and the costume pictures of different classes of society (all Pictorial Charts publications). The chart notes on medieval village life gave detailed information about peasants' work. I also gained much valuable material from the Tower of London Education Service, some of it free of charge. One aid was a large coloured photograph of the Tower today, another a large coloured ground plan and a more sophisticated *Official Chart of the Tower of London.*[13] This last has plans of the Tower and information about victims, warders (Yeoman of the Guard), armourers and the Crown Jewels. It is therefore a very good purchase for many different school uses, and could be cut up and put on coloured card.

The coloured postcard of Richard II from the National Portrait Gallery may be bought cheaply in any quantity and there is also a coloured slide of the same portrait. Other contemporary pictures from the British Library and the Mansell Collection (reproduced in black and white) were invaluable for picture reading. I was also fortunate in being able to make use of Liverpool LEA photocopying machine.

I made a large visual aid of the time-line and the school duplicated separate smaller copies. I also made my own large maps of the revolt in Essex and Kent and London and had smaller copies duplicated. The information for these was found in the books already mentioned.

Workbooks. These were made from coloured sugar paper, large enough to contain A4 worksheets as well as tests, compositions and any illustrations the children wanted to make. They were essential for this class, as all their work was in one book. We looked back to learn from them and this 'visual aid' was a way of securing attention from a very easily distracted and somewhat disturbed class. Some of the children asked for a second book in which to do their own work.

Assessment

No formal assessment was made of this unit of work because of the special nature of this class and the fact that I had to divide them into 'more able' and 'less able'. This very fact means that the unit had failed with this class as a mixed-ability piece of work. Yet the preparation involved in the two sets could be combined and used in a mixed-ability situation. For this activity to be successful in this class, more resources, more experience of group work from the children and greater class control would have been needed. In any case this particular topic, involving concentration on a rapid succession of violent events, lends itself more to class teaching than Unit I did. The available reading material was too advanced for 8 to 9-year-olds, and had to be simplified.

If any progress is to be made in developing skills and understanding of Time, more work has to be attempted in this more formal way before 'discovery methods' can be used. Teachers may be well-advised to use these more class-based lessons in their first attempt at a new topic before they have sized up the reactions of the particular age-group and have collected adequate resources.

These particular children seemed to prefer a teacher-orientated situation which *made* them learn something and involved plenty of short tests and marks. The more able ones were very willing to discuss sensibly and think about the characters, and how they felt, as far back as 1381. The existence of a boy-king and such well-defined characters as Wat Tyler and John Ball clarified the issues for them. They also were good at picture reading. They found that closing their eyes while I *read* a stirring account of events gave them more security than listening to an oral lesson. After the division of the class into two small groups of eight each, they soon adopted my routine of work and most made an effort to co-operate.

References (* indicates suitable for children)

General

R. Hart, *English Life in Chaucer's Day* (Wayland, 1972).

M. Neurath, *They Lived Like This in Chaucer's England* (M. Parrish, 1967).

H. Pluckrose, *Medieval Britain* (Mills and Boon, 1980).

D. Pottinger, *Official Chart of the Tower of London* (Elm Tree Books, 1978).

M. Reeves, *The Medieval Village* (Longman, 1954).

P.A. Sauvain, *Lord and Peasant* Lively History (Hulton, 1970).

* J. Sayers, *At the Time of Geoffrey Chaucer* (Longman, 1977).

D. Taylor, *Chaucer's England* (Dobson, 1968).

* A.F. Titterton, *Work on a Manor* (Ginn, 1954).

Specialised

D. Birt, *The Peasants' Revolt* (Longman, 1974).

* N. Crowther and R. Schofield, *The Peasants' Revolt* Action History (Arnold, 1977).

* L.W. Cowie, *The Black Death and the Peasants' Revolt* (Wayland, 1972).

D. Hill, *The Peasants' Revolt* (Jackdaw no. 36, 1966).

G.R. Kesteven, *The Peasants' Revolt* (Chatto and Windus, 1965).

* W.H. Liddell and R.G.E. Wood, *Essex and the Peasants' Revolt* (Essex Record Office, 1981).

J. Lindsay, *Nine Days' Hero: Wat Tyler* (Dobson, 1964).

M. Price, *The Peasants' Revolt* (Longman, 1980).

M. Price, *Portrait of Britain in the Middle Ages* (OUP, 1951).

H. Priestley, *Swords over Southdowne* (Muller, 1964).

D. Turner, *The Black Death* (Longman, 1978).

Notes

1. History and Social Sciences Teachers' Centre, 377 Clapham Road, London SW9 9BT.

2. Pictorial Charts Educational Trust, 27 Kirchen Road, London W13 0UD.

3. D. Birt, *The Peasants' Revolt* (Longman Resources Unit, 1974), p. 12.

4. J. Sayers, *At the Time of Geoffrey Chaucer* (Longman, 1977), pp. 6-9.

5. A large coloured photograph of the Tower, a ground plan and an official guide.

6. From Froissart's *Chronicle*, in the British Library.

7. See pp. 48-9 for reading pictures.

8. M. Price, *The Peasants' Revolt* (Longman, 1980), pp. 45-7.

9. *Ricardus II,* National Portrait Gallery, no. 565.

10. From the Mansell Collection. Copy in Price, p. 60.

11. From the British Library.

12. Price, pp. 71-88.

13. Don Pottinger, *Official Chart of the Tower of London* (Elm Tree Books, 90 Great Russell Street, London WC1B 3PT, 1978).

BIBLIOGRAPHY

Many detailed references appear at the end of each chapter, and this list merely highlights the most important books, together with extra articles discovered after the relevant chapter of the book was written. It is divided into general books, those useful for Place and Time together, and those specific to either Place or Time.

General

Clift, P. *et al. Record-keeping in Primary Schools* (Macmillan, 1981)

Cooper, K. *Evaluation, Assessment and Record-keeping in History, Geography and Social Science* (Collins/ESL, 1976)

Donaldson, M. *Children's Minds* (Fontana, 1978)

Education 5 to 9: an Illustrative Survey of 80 First Schools (HMSO 1982)

Egan, K. *Educational Development* (OUP, 1979)

Gunning, S. and D., and Wilson, J. *Topic Teaching in the Primary School* (Croom Helm, 1981)

Harries, E. *The New Approach to Social Studies* (London Borough of Merton, 1981)

Heeks, P. *Choosing and Using Books in the First School* (Macmillan, 1981)

ILEA Resources Support Group *The Organisation and Management of Resources in Primary Schools* (ILEA, 1983)

Lane, S.M. and Kemp, M. *An Approach to Topic Work in the Primary School* (Blackie, 1973)

Open University *Living with Children 5-10: A Parent's Guide* (Harper and Row, 1981)

Pollard, M. *Handbook of Resources for Primary Schools* (Ward Lock, 1976)

Rance, P. *Record-keeping in the Progressive Primary School* (Ward Lock 1971)

Tough, J. *Listening to Children Talking* (Ward Lock, 1976)

— *Talking and Learning* (Ward Lock, 1977)

Treasure Chest for Teachers (Teacher Publishing Co., 1978)

Waters, D. *Primary School Projects* (Heinemann, 1982)

Wilson, J. and Gunning, D. 'Focusing Ideas in Junior School Topic Work', *Education 3-13* (Spring 1980).

Place and Time

Avon LEA *History and Geography in Primary Schools* (Avon LEA, 1982)
Blyth, W.A.L. *et al. Place, Time and Society 8-13: Curriculum Planning in History, Geography and Social Studies* (Collins/ESL, 1976)
Birmingham LEA *Further Developments in the Primary Curriculum: Environmental Education* (Birmingham LEA, 1980)
Hopkins, M.F.S. *Learning through the Environment* (Longman, 1968)
Lovett, P. *Local Studies in Towns* (Allen and Unwin, 1980)
Moray House College of Education *An Experiment in Environmental Studies* (Oliver and Boyd, 1968)
Pluckrose, H. *Let's Use the Locality* (Mills and Boon, 1971)
Prosser, P. *The World on Your Doorstep* (McGraw-Hill, 1982)
Scoffham, S. *Using the School's Surroundings: A Guide to Local Studies in Urban Schools* (Ward Lock, 1980)
Timmins, G. (ed.) *Teaching History and Geography in the Primary School: Approaches to Local History* (Preston Polytechnic, 1982)

Place

Barber, H.M.E. and Hayes, J.Y. *Exploring the Physical World with Children 5-9* (Dent, 1973)
Barker, E.J. *The Junior Geography Lesson* (OUP, 1968)
— *Geography and Younger Children* (OUP, 1974)
Barker, R.S. and Garratt, D.J. *Local Studies 5-13: Suggestions for the Non-Specialist Teacher* (Geographical Association, 1982)
Blomberg, I. *It's Easy to Find Your Way* (Swedish Orienteering Association, 1978)
Boardman, D. *Graphicacy and Geography Teaching* (Croom Helm, 1983)
Brown, C.M. 'The Geography Curriculum of the Junior School', *Curriculum*, vol. 2, no. 1 (Spring 1981)
Burden, G.H. (ed.) *Teaching Geography in Junior Schools* (Geographical Association, 1962)
Catling, S. *Your Map Book* (Arnold, 1979)

Catling, S. *Mapwork in Primary and Middle Schools* (Geographical Association, 1981)

Clark, B. (ed.) *The Changing World and the Primary School* (Centre for World Development Education, 1979)

Cracknell, J.R. *Geography through Topics in Primary and Middle Schools* (Geographical Association, 1979)

Cribb, M. *Introducing Maps 5-13* (National Association for Environmental Education, 1982)

DES *New Thinking in School Geography* (HMSO, 1972)

Deverson, H.J. *The Map That Came to Life* (OUP, 1967)

Garnett, O. *Fundamentals of School Geography* (Harrap, 1951)

Harris, M. *Starting from Maps* (Rupert Hart-Davis, 1972)

— *Teachers' Guide* (Rupert Hart-Davis, 1972)

— *Case Studies* (Rupert Hart-Davis, 1972)

ILEA *The Study of Places in the Primary School* (ILEA Guidelines, 1981)

Lynn, S. and Wilson, C. 'Discovering Maps', *Child Education* (May 1980)

Mills, D. (ed.) *Geographical Work in Primary and Middle Schools* (Geographical Association, 1981)

Pemberton, P.H. (ed.) *Geography in Primary Schools* (Geographical Association, 1970)

Scott, N. and Lampitt, R. *Understanding Maps* (Ladybird, 1967)

Storm, M.J. *Playing with Plans* (Longman, 1974)

Williams, T. and Richards, C. 'What Geography do Juniors Learn? An Investigation in Lichfield', *Teaching Geography*, vol. 6, no. 1 (1980)

Time

Best, A.M. *Storytelling: Notes for Teachers of History in the Junior School* (Historical Association, nd)

Blyth, J.E. *History in Primary Schools* (McGraw-Hill, 1982)

Cam, H.M. *Historical Novels* (Historical Association, 1961)

Earl, A. and R. *How Shall I Teach History?* (Blackwell, 1971)

Fairley, J. *Patch History and Creativity* (Longman, 1970)

Hart, T. *Fun with Historical Projects* (Kaye and Ward, 1973)

ILEA *History in the Primary School: Curriculum Guidelines* (ILEA, 1980)

Jamieson, A. *Practical History Teaching* (Evans, 1971)

Johnson, F.J. and Ikin, K.J. *History Fieldwork* (Macmillan, 1974)

Lally, J. and West, J. *The Child's Awareness of the Past: Teachers' Guide* (Hereford and Worcester County History Committee, 1981)

Low-Beer, A. and Blyth, J.E. *Teaching History to Younger Children* (Historical Association, T.H. 52, 1983)

Mays, P. *Why Teach History?* (ULP, 1974)

McBride, G. (ed.) *A Catalogue of Children's Historical Novels* (Queen's University, Belfast, 1976)

Moray House College of Education *History in the Primary School: a Scheme of Work* (Oliver and Boyd, 1965)

Noble, P. *Time-Sense* (Privately published by the author, 1981. See reference 14, Chapter 2 for address)

Pollard, M. *History for Juniors* (Evans, 1973)

Purkis, S. *Oral History in Schools* (Oral History Society, 1980)

Reeves, M. *Why History?* (Longman, 1980)

Rogers, P.J. *The New History: theory into practice* (Historical Association, T.H. 44, 1979)

Steel, D.J. and Taylor, L. *Family History in Schools* (Phillimore, 1973)

Titley, P. *Discovering Local History* (Allman and Sons, 1971)

Unwin, R. *The Visual Dimension in the Study and Teaching of History* (Historical Association, T.H. 49, 1981)

West, J. *History, Here and Now* (Teacher Publishing Co., 1966)

— 'Children's Awareness of the Past', unpublished PhD thesis, Keele University, 1981

INDEX

Blyth, Joan.
Place & time
5-9.

372·89

372·89

Class No.......... .... Acc. No. 86649..........

Place and Time with Children Five to Nine

JOAN BLYTH

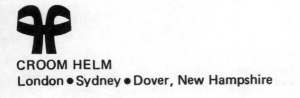

CROOM HELM
London • Sydney • Dover, New Hampshire

©1984 J.E. Blyth
Croom Helm Ltd., Provident House, Burrell Row,
Beckenham, Kent BR3 1AT
Croom Helm Australia Pty Ltd, First Floor, 139 King Street,
Sydney, NSW 2001, Australia

Croom Helm, 51 Washington Street, Dover,
New Hampshire 03820, USA

British Library Cataloguing in Publication Data

Blyth, Joan
    Place and time with children five to
    nine.—(Croom Helm teaching 5-13 series)
    1. Middle schools—England
    I. Title
    373.2'36   LA635

    ISBN 0-7099-0661-7
    ISBN 0-7099-0662-5 Pbk

Printed and bound in Great Britain
by Billing & Sons Limited, Worcester.

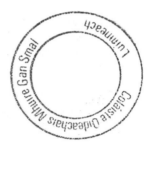

PLACE AND TIME WITH CHILDREN FIVE TO NINE

CROOM HELM TEACHING 5-13 SERIES

Edited by COLIN RICHARDS,
formerly of the School of Education, Leicester University

ASSESSMENT IN PRIMARY AND MIDDLE SCHOOLS
Marten Shipman

ORGANISING LEARNING IN THE
PRIMARY SCHOOL CLASSROOM
Joan Dean

DEVELOPMENT, EXPERIENCE AND CURRICULUM
IN PRIMARY EDUCATION
W.A.L. Blyth